Journalism

Other Books of Related Interest

Opposing Viewpoints Series

Mass Media

Media Violence

Privacy

At Issue Series

Are Books Becoming Extinct?

What Is the Future of the Music Industry?

What Is the Impact of Twitter?

Current Controversies Series

Media Ethics

Politics and Media

Violence in the Media

"Congress shall make
no law . . . abridging
the freedom of speech,
or of the press."

First Amendment to the US Constitution

The basic foundation of our democracy is the First Amendment guarantee of freedom of expression. The Opposing Viewpoints Series is dedicated to the concept of this basic freedom and the idea that it is more important to practice it than to enshrine it.

OPPOSING VIEWPOINTS® SERIES

I Journalism

Roman Espejo, book editor

GREENHAVEN PRESS
A part of Gale, Cengage Learning

GALE
CENGAGE Learning·

Farmington Hills, Mich • San Francisco • New York • Waterville, Maine
Meriden, Conn • Mason, Ohio • Chicago

Elizabeth Des Chenes, *Director, Content Strategy*
Douglas Dentino, Manager, *New Product*

© 2014 Greenhaven Press, a part of Gale, Cengage Learning.

WCN: 01-100-101

Gale and Greenhaven Press are registered trademarks used herein under license.

For more information, contact:
Greenhaven Press
27500 Drake Rd.
Farmington Hills, MI 48331-3535
Or you can visit our Internet site at gale.cengage.com

LIBRARY OF CONGRESS CATALOGING-IN-PUBLICATION DATA

Journalism / Roman Espejo, book editor.
    p. cm. -- (Opposing viewpoints)
    Includes bibliographical references and index.
    ISBN 978-0-7377-6955-5 (hardcover) -- ISBN 978-0-7377-6956-2 (paperback)
    1. Journalism--History--21st century. I. Espejo, Roman, 1977- editor of compilation.
    PN4815.2.J67 2014
    070.909'05--dc23
                                                            2013047498

Printed in the United States of America
1 2 3 4 5 6 7 18 17 16 15 14

Contents

Chapter 3: How Should Journalists Be Protected?

Chapter 4: What Is the Future of Journalism?

Why Consider Opposing Viewpoints?

> *"The only way in which a human being can make some approach to knowing the whole of a subject is by hearing what can be said about it by persons of every variety of opinion and studying all modes in which it can be looked at by every character of mind. No wise man ever acquired his wisdom in any mode but this."*
>
> *John Stuart Mill*

In our media-intensive culture it is not difficult to find differing opinions. Thousands of newspapers and magazines and dozens of radio and television talk shows resound with differing points of view. The difficulty lies in deciding which opinion to agree with and which "experts" seem the most credible. The more inundated we become with differing opinions and claims, the more essential it is to hone critical reading and thinking skills to evaluate these ideas. Opposing Viewpoints books address this problem directly by presenting stimulating debates that can be used to enhance and teach these skills. The varied opinions contained in each book examine many different aspects of a single issue. While examining these conveniently edited opposing views, readers can develop critical thinking skills such as the ability to compare and contrast authors' credibility, facts, argumentation styles, use of persuasive techniques, and other stylistic tools. In short, the Opposing Viewpoints Series is an ideal way to attain the higher-level thinking and reading skills so essential in a culture of diverse and contradictory opinions.

In addition to providing a tool for critical thinking, Opposing Viewpoints books challenge readers to question their own strongly held opinions and assumptions. Most people form their opinions on the basis of upbringing, peer pressure, and personal, cultural, or professional bias. By reading carefully balanced opposing views, readers must directly confront new ideas as well as the opinions of those with whom they disagree. This is not to argue simplistically that everyone who reads opposing views will—or should—change his or her opinion. Instead, the series enhances readers' understanding of their own views by encouraging confrontation with opposing ideas. Careful examination of others' views can lead to the readers' understanding of the logical inconsistencies in their own opinions, perspective on why they hold an opinion, and the consideration of the possibility that their opinion requires further evaluation.

Evaluating Other Opinions

To ensure that this type of examination occurs, Opposing Viewpoints books present all types of opinions. Prominent spokespeople on different sides of each issue as well as well-known professionals from many disciplines challenge the reader. An additional goal of the series is to provide a forum for other, less known, or even unpopular viewpoints. The opinion of an ordinary person who has had to make the decision to cut off life support from a terminally ill relative, for example, may be just as valuable and provide just as much insight as a medical ethicist's professional opinion. The editors have two additional purposes in including these less known views. One, the editors encourage readers to respect others' opinions—even when not enhanced by professional credibility. It is only by reading or listening to and objectively evaluating others' ideas that one can determine whether they are worthy of consideration. Two, the inclusion of such viewpoints encourages the important critical thinking skill of objectively evaluating an author's credentials and bias. This evaluation will illuminate an author's reasons for taking a particular stance on an issue and will aid in readers' evaluation of the author's ideas.

It is our hope that these books will give readers a deeper understanding of the issues debated and an appreciation of the complexity of even seemingly simple issues when good and honest people disagree. This awareness is particularly important in a democratic society such as ours in which people enter into public debate to determine the common good. Those with whom one disagrees should not be regarded as enemies but rather as people whose views deserve careful examination and may shed light on one's own.

Thomas Jefferson once said that "difference of opinion leads to inquiry, and inquiry to truth." Jefferson, a broadly educated man, argued that "if a nation expects to be ignorant and free . . . it expects what never was and never will be." As individuals and as a nation, it is imperative that we consider the opinions of others and examine them with skill and discernment. The Opposing Viewpoints Series is intended to help readers achieve this goal.

David L. Bender and Bruno Leone,
Founders

Introduction

"Defamation is one of the greatest legal dangers for anyone who earns a living with words and images."
—Mark Hanna and Mike Dodd, editors of McNae's Essential Law for Journalists

With print, broadcast, and Internet platforms, journalists have the power to reveal wrongdoings and inequalities in government, business, and society. However, if a published or broadcasted statement is false, journalists can be held liable for the resulting harm and sued for defamation. If the false statement is written, it is libel. If the statement is spoken, it is slander. In the United States, defamation cases are decided in civil courts, and punishment takes the form of damages, usually monetary awards. "The government can't imprison someone for making a defamatory statement since it is not a crime," according to FindLaw, a legal website. "Instead, defamation is considered to be a civil wrong, or a tort. A person that has suffered a defamatory statement may sue the person that made the statement under defamation law."[1] However, about half of the states have criminal libel statutes.

Libel is of main concern to journalists and reporters. In short, it is the defamation of character published to a third party—readers and viewers—that harms the reputation of the subject, which can be a person, business, organization, or product. Libel laws vary from state to state but share some similarities in legal systems nationwide. "Generally, courts consider six different legal elements in libel cases: the defamatory nature of the communication, how it was published, the truth or falsity of the claims, whether it is 'of and concerning' an individual, reputational harm caused, and the degree of fault,"[2] according to the Reporters Committee for Freedom of the Press (RCFP).

A defamatory statement exposes the subject to hatred, ridicule, and contempt, which causes him or her to be shunned or harms a personal or professional reputation. According to the RCFP, "Courts generally are required to take the full context of a publication into account when determining whether the publication is defamatory."[3] Nonetheless, the RCFP advises that a single headline, drawing, or photograph can be libelous. A statement that is "privileged," such as testimony given in court, is not actionable even if it is false and derogatory.

Publication of a defamatory statement can be intentional or unintentional. "The media can be liable for the republication of a libelous statement made by another person or entity but quoted in a news article,"[4] asserts the RCFP. In fact, the RCFP warns that a publication can be sued if it publishes a letter to the editor or advertisement containing a false statement or unproven allegation.

As for the truth or falsity of the claim, minor inaccuracies do not make a statement automatically libelous as long as it is substantially true. Opinions, moreover, are not usually actionable, because they cannot be proven to be objectively false. Still, the RCFP suggests that a quotation that is altered or inaccurate that harms the reputation of the quoted person can be actionable. And in the United States, the burden of proof in libel cases falls on the plaintiff, or the subject of the statement. Previously, under common law, the burden of proof fell on the defendant, until the US Supreme Court changed the standard in several cases. This includes *Philadelphia Newspapers, Inc. v. Hepps* (1986), which found that a private party must bear the burden of proof in a libel suit against a newspaper.

The "of or concerning" principle, as described by the RCFP, is that no liability exists if the statement is not proven to be "of or concerning" the subject. For example, government bodies and groups with more than twenty-five people cannot sue for libel. "However, if the statement at issue can be interpreted as referring to a particular person in a group, that person can sue. Also, if the offending information pertains to a majority of the members of a small group, any member of the group has standing to sue,"[5] the RCFP maintains. Additionally, a business can sue if the defamatory statement places its practices, integrity, or finances under fire.

The courts must also consider the reputational harm caused by the defamatory statement published in the media. Depending on the state, if the statement is about the subject's personal history (e.g., health, sexual behavior), criminal record, profession, or business, then harm is presumed and does not need to be shown, says the RCFP. "In most states, damage to reputation also is presumed when accusations of fraud, incompetence, or improper behavior are made about business or professional people,"[6] the group adds.

Determining the degree of fault depends on whether the subject is a public figure, public official, or private figure. A public figure is a celebrity, and a public official is a high-ranking or powerful government official. But the definition of a public or private figure is not always straightforward. For instance, a noted vaccine expert may be considered a public figure in the debate about vaccine effectiveness but only for that purpose. As determined by the US Supreme Court in *New York Times Co. v. Sullivan* (1964), public officials and public figures have to prove actual malice to win damages in a libel suit. Private figures only have to prove negligence. "'Actual malice' in libel parlance, does not mean ill will or intent to harm. Instead, it means the defendant knew that the challenged statements were false or acted with reckless disregard for the truth," asserts the RCFP. How journalists gather information, research a story, or edit quotations may be investigated. "Although carelessness is not usually considered reckless disregard, ignoring obvious methods of substantiating allegations could be considered reckless,"[7] according to the RCFP.

Defamation and libel are two of the many issues debated in journalistic ethics and standards. Other dilemmas and debates—from plagiarism to the integrity of undercover reporting—are recurring concerns for many journalists, editors, and news organizations. Furthermore, the Internet and digital technology are transforming the media landscape, challenging the business models of print newspapers and magazines. *Opposing Viewpoints: Journalism* probes these topics and more under the following chapter headings: "What Are the Ethical Issues Facing Journalism?," "How Should Journalism Be Practiced?," "How Should Journalists Be Protected?," and "What Is the Future of Journalism?" The contrasting positions and impassioned views compiled in this anthology attest to journalism's vital role in a democratic society.

Notes

1. FindLaw, "Defamation Law: The Basics." http://injury.findlaw.com/torts-and -personal-injuries/defamation-law-the-basics.html.

2. Reporters Committee for Freedom of the Press, "Digital Journalist's Legal Guide," 7th ed. www.rcfp.org/digital-journalists-legal-guide/libel.

3. Reporters Committee for Freedom of the Press, *The First Amendment Handbook*. www.rcfp.org/rcfp/orders/docs/FAHB.pdf.

4. Reporters Committee for Freedom of the Press, *The First Amendment Handbook*.

5. Reporters Committee for Freedom of the Press, *The First Amendment Handbook*.

6. Reporters Committee for Freedom of the Press, *The First Amendment Handbook*.

7. Reporters Committee for Freedom of the Press, *The First Amendment Handbook*.

OPPOSING
VIEWPOINTS®
SERIES

CHAPTER 1

What Are the Ethical Issues Facing Journalism?

Chapter Preface

In June 2012 Paresh Jha, a reporter for Connecticut's *New Canaan News*, was fired for fabricating facts. In the two years that he had worked for the newspaper, Jha had made up quotes and sources for twenty-five stories. The Connecticut Society of Professional Journalists subsequently stripped Jha of one of two awards it had presented to him in 2011 for journalism excellence. "Paresh Jha is not the first journalist who was discovered fabricating content presented as journalism. Unfortunately, he likely will not be the last," stated journalism professor Roy S. Gutterman in a review of Jha's award-winning stories. "He is also not the first journalist to submit fictional accounts to an award competition and subsequently win a prestigious award."[1]

The same month that the *New Canaan News* fired Jha, the *Wall Street Journal* fired intern Liane Membis for fabricating material in three stories. Then in July 2012 came the revelation that journalist and author Jonah Lerner, then on the staff of the prestigious *New Yorker* magazine, had falsely quoted musician Bob Dylan in his best-selling book *Imagine: How Creativity Works*. Lerner resigned from the magazine, and the book's publisher pulled the book from store shelves and halted further shipments. Also in July 2012 Sun Times Media fired photographer Tamara Bell for using fake names and quotes with twenty-two photographs that had appeared in several news publications.

Journalism professionals, of course, decry fabrication. "Under no circumstances should a journalist fill in even the slightest gap in a story, even with a logical presumption," argues Steve Buttry, digital transformation editor at Digital Media

---

1. Roy S. Gutterman, "Connecticut Society of Professional Journalists Independent Review of Select Contest Entries," July 26, 2012. http://connecticutspj.org/wp-content/uploads/2012/07/CTSPJ-Independent-Review-Revised.pdf.

First and a journalism trainer and consultant. "Fabrication does not come in degrees any more than virginity or death come in degrees. Make up a tiny fact that probably is close to the truth to fill a small gap in a story and you've taken the first step on a path that will lead to bigger lies and eventual discovery and disgrace,"[2] he explains. Nonetheless, others point out that reliance on the practice attests to the problems facing reporters and journalists working in a competitive news cycle accelerated by digital media. "This whole profession of journalism is all about pressure, deadlines and being the first, best, and most-clicked on. And the temptation to cut corners is always there," suggests Alexander Abad-Santos, writing for The Wire website. He speculates that mixed messages about the craft of reporting abound in the news industry as well, noting, "It's even more confusing when you have hero-editors like *The New Yorker's* David Remnick telling you that committing a 'journalistic misdemeanor' here and there won't necessarily get you into trouble."[3] The authors in this chapter debate the ethical issues that journalists face.

2. Steve Buttry, "Our Cheating Culture: Plagiarism and Fabrication Are Unacceptable in Journalism," *The Buttry Diary* (blog), October 31, 2011. http://stevebuttry.wordpress .com/2011/10/31/our-cheating-culture-plagiarism-and-fabrication-are-unacceptable -in-journalism/.
3. Alexander Abad-Santos, "Fabrication Is This Week's Crime Against Journalism," The Wire, June 26, 2012. www.thewire.com/business/2012/06/fabrication-weeks-crime -against-journalism/53943.

| "We should stop pretending that objectivity is possible, and stop asking our news providers to practice it."

Objectivity in Journalism Is a Myth

Theodore Dawes

In the following viewpoint, Theodore Dawes argues that objectivity in journalism—a plain, unbiased restatement of the facts—is nonexistent. He maintains that the decisions of reporters and editors to select particular quotes from interviews, to summarize conversations or actions, and to determine what is newsworthy are all editorially subjective. Dawes also contends that providing contrasting perspectives about a subject to create a "balanced" and "objective" story is based on the illogical assumption that the truth lies somewhere between the two perspectives. He concludes that objectivity is a pretense for propagandizing readers without their awareness and must be abandoned in journalism as a principle and an expectation. Theodore Dawes is a reporter and writer based in Alabama.

As you read, consider the following questions:

1. According to Dawes, what extremes do journalists take to balance both sides of a story?

Theodore Dawes, "Why the News Makes You Angry," *American Thinker*, June 26, 2010.

2. What example does the author provide to illustrate his position that facts are useless in determining what is newsworthy without a moral basis?

3. Where does the notion of objectivity in journalism originate, according to Dawes?

Some time ago, a general manager of the Associated Press, the massive news collective, opined on the importance of "objectivity" in reporting, calling it the Holy Grail of journalism.

He's right, but only in the sense that objectivity is the source and substance of a massive mythology. In fact, there is no such thing as objective reporting. Unfortunately, that has never stopped those who engage in journalism from claiming not only that it exists, but that they practice it.

Objectivity, in the journalistic definition, is a bare-boned restatement of facts, e.g., he said this, she said that. But by the time the reporter gets around to transcribing comments, he has already made a number of decisions, including perhaps the most important one: Is this subject sufficiently compelling to justify my effort and the requisite newsprint or broadcast time?

In fact, there is simply no way to establish objectively what is important and what isn't. The reporter and the editors have to make that decision. Then the reporter, restrained by available column inches (or face time on a broadcast), must pare down the conversation or action, usually by summarizing it. This introduces another layer of subjectivity.

And on, and on, and on.

Both Sides of the Story

But! you may be saying to yourself. Can't we at least get both sides of the story?

Well, yes, if both sides are compelling. It's called balance, and it assumes the truth lies somewhere in the middle. Unfortunately, there is no basis in logic for assuming any such thing, and so it has, naturally, been carried to extremes. Though I've never found strong evidence of the event, there is an urban legend that at least one reporter, in the interest of balance, gave equal time to a rapist to give his side of the story. The tale is often used to illustrate the absurd lengths to which "objectivity" by the press could be taken.

There are more concrete examples. During the first Iraq War [also known as the Persian Gulf War of 1990–1991], CNN reporter Peter Arnett was widely criticized for reporting on Operation Desert Storm [the U.S. military invasion of Iraq] from Baghdad, where he was fed propaganda daily by the government of [Iraqi dictator] Saddam Hussein. In a later television interview, Arnett was asked, "If there was information you could have gotten out that could have saved scores, hundreds of American lives, you wouldn't have transmitted that information?"

Arnett replied, "I would not have transmitted it. I was in Baghdad because I was a correspondent for CNN, which has no political affiliations with the U.S. government, thank goodness." Objectivity would have required him to stand by and watch American soldiers die.

If you think his stance was unusual, you're right. If you think it's unheard of, think again. Michael Schudson, a professor at the University of California, San Diego, has written a number of respected and widely quoted essays on objectivity in journalism. In one, he said:

> "Objectivity" is at once a moral ideal, a set of reporting and editing practices, and an observable pattern of news writing. Its presence can therefore be identified by several measures:
>
> (a) journalists' express allegiance to the norm—in speeches, conferences, formal codes of professional ethics, textbooks in journalism education, debates and discussions in professional journals, and scientific surveys of journalists'opinions. [...]

23

Arnett simply spoke for those modern journalists who hold "objectivity" as the highest calling. He felt no obligation to act morally—in any sense of the word you or I might recognize—because he had a higher moral ideal, which is objectivity, which is by definition amoral.

If that sounds paradoxical, that's because it is.

Determining What Is Newsworthy

It's also remarkably dumb. After all, without some moral basis, facts are useless in determining what is newsworthy.

Consider: A bomb exploded.

Or: A bomb exploded in a day care center.

The first is meaningless data, while the second outrages the moral sense and thus becomes a story. Determining what is newsworthy requires judgment, and that's why the news is always, in small ways and large, a product of the reporter's very subjective viewpoint.

To illustrate the point, let's reconsider the rape story I earlier mentioned, using it as a kind of thought experiment:

Let's say you were a reporter for the local daily [newspaper], and you took the call from the young woman who said she was raped. She tells you it took place at a college party, and her rape was abetted by many of the young men in attendance at the party. Would you then interview the alleged rapist to hear his side of the story?

What if it took place at Duke University, and he was a Lacrosse team member [a controversial case from 2006]?

The simple fact is, objectivity is useless at determining what is news, and how it should be covered. That requires judgment, not math.

A Fairly New Concept

The concept of journalistic objectivity is fairly new. For our first centuries, most newspapers in the U.S. were partisan, serving the political or religious parties that financed them.

Objectivity in Journalism

Objectivity is judgement based on observable phenomena and uninfluenced by emotions or personal prejudices. In writing, objectivity is the absence of the writer's opinion or feeling about the subject matter. So much so that academic writing has developed a preference for the use of the third person to refer to the author of the work in an attempt to give a false sense of objectivity to writing. References such as "the researcher", "the author" and "the experimenter" abound in academic writing. In many other instances, the passive voice is used and abused—things happen on their own without an agency. It is known in psychology that when one refers to oneself in the third person, chances are that such reference indicates the presence of a psychological disorder.

Ali Darwish,
A Journalist's Guide to Live Direct
and Unbiased News Translation, *2010.*

H.S. Stansaas, writing in *Journal of Mass Media Sciences*, said it took until 1904 for objective journalism to become commonplace, and only by 1925 had the practice been established as the norm.

No one can say with certainty where the notion of objectivity came from or how it became an ethical imperative, but it almost certainly had something to do with money. Some say the primary impetus was the introduction of the telegraph, which introduced the delivery of news over long distances (the news wires). The stories had to be palatable to those in both Seattle [in the Pacific Northwest] and in Sewanee [Tennessee, in the South]. Certainly in the age of three television networks [ABC, CBS, and NBC], objectivity—defined as un-objectionable to all—was the only business model that made sense.

It is also largely an American invention. Following the re-cent elections in Great Britain, essayist Paola Totaro penned the obituary for objectivity in the British press. Addressing her readers, Totaro said,

> "The British media have always been politically aligned, worn their colours on their sleeves. I hear you cry. Yes, true. But never has the bias been so obvious, so untrammelled, so utterly and completely fearless."

A Trick of Perspective

Most conservatives call for more objective reporting. They are completely accurate in declaring the MSM [mainstream me-dia] is almost wholly biased to the left. But here is where things get a little sticky. Those on the far left (see the *Nation* [magazine], for example) claim the MSM is tilted to the right. They are also correct.

Boston Globe columnist Jeff Jacoby recently provided a nice overview of the "lack of ideological diversity" found within most American newsrooms, describing "the reflexive support for Democrats, the distaste for religion and the mili-tary, the cheerleading for liberal enthusiasms from gun control to gay marriage[.]"

Those on the far left, however, say the major media com-panies are shills [promoters] for the country's biggest corpo-rations, primarily because they are so beholden to them—and are, in fact, mostly owned by them. They're absolutely right.

Let's do another thought experiment. Let's say you're the anchor of the lowest-rated evening network news broadcast. You're nevertheless making $15 million a year, which you know is more than the entire combined budgets for NPR's [National Public Radio's] *Morning Edition* and *All Things Con-*

sidered. Handlers dress you. Important people buddy up to you. And somewhere, in your heart of hearts, you know your only real talent is that you're cute as a bug. . . .

And yet, many people, particularly those in the press corps, deny that there is bias. Conservatives and leftists both say this is self-serving nonsense, and disingenuous at best. Some dishonesty is in play, but there is another mechanism at work, a kind of optical illusion. Call it a trick of perspective.

When conservatives read the *New York Times*, they can see that the underlying assumptions of the reporters are basically those outlined by Jacoby in his *Boston Globe* essay. When those on the far left read it, they are frustrated to see capitalism as the working assumption of the American polity.

But when a *New York Times* reporter reads the story, he sees objective truth, because he shares his colleague's underlying assumptions. The assumptions disappear, as if by magic, because it is only in conflict that you can recognize someone else's bias.

Why the News Makes You Angry

Okay, we've now established that journalistic objectivity is 1) a new idea, 2) a bad idea, and 3) impossible.

So what do we do next?

We should stop pretending that objectivity is possible, and stop asking our news providers to practice it.

That might sound shocking, but it may be easier to accept if we properly define our current system. We're indebted to the remarkable Marvin Olasky, who has provided exactly that. Olasky, a former journalism professor at the University of Texas and now editor of *World* magazine, says journalists today engage in "disguised subjectivity." In reality, it isn't objectivity at all, or even the effort to come close. Instead, Olasky says, it involves the practice of "strategic ritual," which he describes as "the process of selecting sources and structuring quotes so that a reporter may advance his view in the news story while claiming objectivity."

Sound familiar?

In his comment, Olasky provides the key reason why we need to abandon all notions of objectivity. It is in fact the perfect mechanism for slipping ideas and opinions into news stories while leaving readers unaware they are being propagandized. Under cover of "objectivity," the nation's reporters and editors are providing us not with the truth, but rather with the facts, the quotes, and the views they want us to hear, read, and believe.

Of course, if you are unaware you are being propagandized—if you actually believe you're reading the objective truth—then you are most likely to believe it.

It's the old primrose path, don't you know. And that's why the news makes you angry.

| "Objectivity, far from a device of old media or the elite, is the key to deeply democratic news media now and in the future."

Objectivity in Journalism Must Be Pursued

Aidan White

In the following viewpoint, Aidan White maintains that while critics view objectivity as elitist, overly dependent on balance, or impossible to achieve, it is valuable to journalistic practice. He contends that objective journalism is highly democratic, bringing reliable, concise, and timely information to consumers. White concludes that objectivity does not require that all perspectives— even illegitimate views—be equally presented, as newsrooms are capable of dealing with disputed facts. Aidan White is a journalist and the director of the Ethical Journalism Network, an international association for journalists and media organizations that promotes ethics, good governance, and independent regulation of media content.

As you read, consider the following questions:

1. According to White, what does objective journalism set out to establish?

Aidan White, "Journalism's Era of Change, but Objectivity Still Plays a Critical Role," *Ethical Journalism Network*, January 15, 2013. Copyright © 2013 by Ethical Journalism Network. All rights reserved. Reproduced by permission.

2. What is the author's position on objectivity and human emotion?

3. What is the core value of objectivity, according to White?

That everyone understands objectivity differently makes it a dangerously fuzzy concept, easy road kill in the rush to new journalistic techniques.

We dismiss it at our peril.

At heart, objective journalism sets out to establish the facts about a situation, report fairly the range of opinion around it and take a first cut at what arguments are the most reasonable. To keep the presentation rigorous, journalists should have professional reporting and editing skills (be they staff or independent journalists, paid or unpaid). To show their commitment to balance, journalists should keep their personal opinions to themselves.

It's a simple enough concept, distillable to "unbiased journalism," "trusted reporting" or in the view of some, simply "journalism."

Add to that "customer service." The news consumer needs faith that there's somewhere to go quickly for the basic facts that business, politics and personal safety depend on.

Is [Libyan dictator Muammar] Gaddafi dead? Is the [BP *Deep Horizon* oil well still leaking? How close to the [leaking] Fukushima [nuclear] reactor [in Japan] can I safely go? It seems a no-brainer that there's a value to established, reliable voices on the things that matter most—experienced in sorting out contradictions, wary of sloppiness and hoaxes and not pushing a personal objective.

Yet attach the word "objective" to the concept, and confusion ensues.

To some, objectivity somehow evokes the "legacy" news industry, destined to die with it (a demise as yet unobserved, if accepted by many as an article of faith). These critics see objectivity as a reactive, stenographic form of journalism, so wedded to "balance" that it cannot distinguish between legitimate and lunatic opinion, between scientific truth and trash.

Others see objectivity as the calling card of the elite, rooted in a belief that "professionals" can so completely cover a complex story that journalists' voices are all people need to hear.

Still others believe objectivity has never existed at all because perfect objectivity is impossible. Much like a perfect vacuum or a perfect circle, it can be imagined but never really created, so its loss is without cost.

Our view is that objectivity, far from a device of old media or the elite, is the key to deeply democratic news media now and in the future. It can reliably serve both traditional journalism and new models, including the most open-sourced processes for gathering and analyzing news.

Perfect objectivity is indeed hard to imagine. (We mean it in the sense of presenting all sides of an issue, not of determining a single, objective truth.) The very act of deciding what angles of a story to cover is inherently subjective, notes [public communications professor] Gilles Gauthier of [Canada's] Laval University. Where and how to point the camera comes from personal instinct and feelings, not mathematical formulas. Getting "both sides of the story" can leave journalists satisfied they've done a good day's work when even more valid third and fourth sides remain unexplored.

More Practical than Ever

Yet we live with a system of courts that is not perfectly just and we accept rides in cars from people who are not perfect drivers. We play by the percentages in everything. And the percentages favoring objective journalism have actually increased in the past couple of decades [1993–2013]. For those who believe objective reporting is a worthy concept but a problem in practice, crowdsourcing and social networks now make it more practical than ever.

Today's objective journalism does not have to consist solely of words and images from journalists. Crowdsourcing of information and policy alternatives, through the news media's own platforms or social networks, can be integral parts of an objective journalistic process. Of course, the crowd must reflect a variety of points of view; crowdsourcing among members of a mob will bring a plethora of voices but not of viewpoints.

There is no contradiction between professionals doing their own reporting while also curating the voices of others. This has been the story of the civil war in Syria. International news organizations have sent their own correspondents into Syria and broken their own stories. But the same organizations have crowdsourced a huge amount of day-to-day battle-front coverage, using social networks and direct contacts to obtain details, photos and even live video of street battles. The authentic voice of Syrian individuals reporting from the scene has vastly enriched the picture without endangering the objectivity of the product; the organizations involved have long experience in identifying skilled reporters and detecting fake and outdated footage.

Is such crowdsourced reporting ultimately a threat to professional journalists? We think not, because objectivity isn't so much about controlling the information available as making sure it's all there. Whether a conflict is on a distant battlefield or in a state legislature, there is no contradiction between the voices of those at the scene and of journalists, detached from the event but close to news consumers, putting the pieces into a whole that will command their audience's attention. And, of course, sometimes journalists can be on the scene and present the big picture at the same time. . . .

Then there's a whole additional world of reader reactions. New, professional media like the *Huffington Post* have invested significant resources in that feedback. The result is an even more objective account of events that now takes in people at the scene, detached and professional observers and the opinions of the readership at large.

Summarizing the News

On breaking stories, journalists carry out another, supremely important role: summarizing the news and the debate at frequent intervals—sometimes minute by minute—for those who cannot follow every turn of the story. Those who see journalists as elite "gatekeepers" under such circumstances have the picture precisely backward.

It is a far more elite perspective to think that the majority of the world's population has the time or inclination to follow in detail every story that interests them. It is an elite concept that in a future world without "objective journalism," a person who hears on the way to work that [Palestinian militant Islamist group] Hamas is firing rockets at Israel will arrive at work, head immediately to his personal, well-curated Twitter feed of conflicting voices and video from Israel and Gaza and distill his own, exquisitely balanced version of events.

Most people who arrive at work need to start work. They value fast, concise and reliable news when their time permits. Objective media provide a profoundly democratic source of information, offering the vast majority of the population with limited time and attention an account of the world in a fashion that news consumers have long found quick and reliable. This is a competitive advantage of "legacy" media that helps explain its continued existence at a time of so many challenges.

It is no surprise then that, as the Project for Excellence in Journalism [now known as the Pew Research Journalism Project] has found, so many social media posts link to traditional objective media. Or that breaking news on Twitter tends to be massively retweeted only once it's confirmed by a traditional news organization; *American Journalism Review* found

A New Notion of Objectivity

The best option is to reform objectivity to meet valid criticisms and preserve important practices of objective reporting. Without a thoughtful reform of objectivity, we risk losing a much-needed ethical restraint on today's news media. What we require is a progressive and philosophically sophisticated notion of objectivity that corrects stubborn misconceptions that have deep historical roots. We need a notion of objectivity that reflects our current understandings of knowledge and inquiry. The ideal of objectivity, properly understood, is vital not only for responsible journalism but for responsible scientific inquiry, informed public deliberations, and fair ethical and legal judgments. The peculiar Western attempt to be objective is a long, honourable tradition that is part of our continuing struggle to discern significant, well-grounded truths and to make fair decisions.

Stephen J.A. Ward, Invention of Journalism Ethics: The Path to Objectivity and Beyond, *2001.*

the case of Whitney Houston's death a good example. Social network users, once they learn of a breaking story, massively seek out traditional sources for more information and imagery.

Not Equating Truth and Nonsense

What about the claim that covering both sides of the story leads objective journalists to equate truth and nonsense?

[Professor] Clay Shirky of New York University says, "Judgement about legitimate consensus is becoming a critical journalistic skill, one that traditional training and mores don't prepare most practitioners for." [Craigslist founder] Craig

Newmark fears that a "pretense of objectivity" leads journalists to treat fringe beliefs as significantly as facts in an effort to show the story is reporting all points of view.

As Aidan White of the Ethical Journalism Network puts it, "To be ethical, journalists, particularly those covering politics, must stop quoting two sides of a story when one side is lying. At the very least they must tell their audience when that side is lying."

In fact, modern newsrooms have been pushing back at this limited view of objectivity for some time. Legions of aggressive, objective journalists do not share [late, iconic journalist] Arthur Brisbane's puzzlement over whether it is possible "to be objective and fair when the reporter is choosing to correct one fact over another."

Objective newsrooms today deal regularly and quite successfully with disputes over facts. Since the vast majority of the world's scientists believe the globe is heating up, few news stories on the subject devote substantial space to those who deny it. Fact-checking politicians' statements originated with traditional, objective media, and flourished there long before the current wave of new-media sites doing the same thing on an expanded basis.

If a journalist has thoroughly studied a subject and understands it well, the tenets of objectivity do not require a "view from nowhere" that ignores the journalist's knowledge. On social networks, he can rebut false information with facts. . . .

Objectivity also doesn't mean rejection of human emotion. The slaying of children by a gunman at a school can be fairly referred to as horrific; there is no need for a paragraph saying "on the other hand." A photographer covering a war or disaster can put his camera aside when he has a chance to save a life. A journalist can be transparent about his biography and experiences, so long as he doesn't turn them into a political agenda. There is nothing robotic about an objective journalist; reasonable judgments and human ethics and experience need not be suppressed.

Objective Journalism and Wikipedia

The attraction of objective journalism is such that Wikipedia, increasingly a destination for breaking news coverage, has adopted a policy of presenting an objective, "neutral point of view."

When a big story happens, Wikipedia readers post thousands of updates. Volunteer editors quickly join the effort, organizing the material. Yet as [social media researcher] Brian Keegan discovered, the editors change from one breaking news story to another and few have substantial editing experience. According to Keegan, who conducted research at Northwestern University's Medill School of Communications: "In all likelihood, readers of these breaking news articles are mostly consuming the work of editors who have never previously worked on this kind of event. In other words, some of the earliest and most widely read information about breaking news events is written by people with fewer journalistic qualifications than Medill freshmen."

Here is a situation where a pillar of new media values objectivity, but professional standards or qualifications could make that goal even more attainable. It should also be noted that the heaviest lifting in Wikipedia's "coverage" of breaking news is often not being done by its contributors or editors. It is being done by the traditional media, from which much of the information being curated is taken. If Wikipedia's contributors couldn't count on these reports being objective to begin with, Wikipedia would have difficulty living up to its "neutral point of view."

Wikipedia's policy aside, it's surprising that amid the success of many new media that value objectivity, few generally accepted codes of conduct have emerged. Despite some laudable attempts, the best examples of new journalism have failed to unite around consistent ethics codes to the degree that legacy media have. Work now under way suggests a desire for progress in this direction. But sometimes such efforts are undertaken in the same breath as pronouncing traditional journalism dead or dying, complicating the import of some of its most useful principles.

The Core Value of Objectivity

The value objective journalists add goes well beyond getting individual stories right. It goes to the entire texture of information in a society.

In some social systems, the news media serve the state; [Communist Russian revolutionary leader] Vladimir Lenin called the press a collective agitator, propagandist and organizer for the Soviet system. Elsewhere, media exist to serve the politics of individual owners, or to foment sensation for the sake of profit.

Happily, civilized society has also allowed the rise of voices of reason that can assess a situation from everyone's viewpoint and lead rational discussion. If the discussion leaders focus on the merits of all sides instead of proclaiming an agenda of their own, the discussion is more successful.

This is the core value of objectivity: the creation of a strong, balanced public dialogue that cannot be overwhelmed by government fiat, political slant, specious information, simplistic argument and hate.

In Nigeria, [former government official] Mallam Nasir El-Rufai asks, "What happens when every sense of objectivity is blurred by the murky ink of hatchet writers or clouded by shades of religious and ethnic prisms? What happens when voices without conscience, and loath to accept facts dominate our media and discourse?"

The value of objectivity is not simply a debate to hold in seminars and journalism schools. It is a fundamental value of public discourse and collaboration. It will endure precisely as long as people speak out in its defence.

| *"Going undercover has proved to be an indispensable tool in the high-value, high-impact journalism of changing systems and righting wrongs."*

Undercover Journalism Is Justified

Brooke Kroeger

In the following viewpoint, Brooke Kroeger asserts that undercover reporting exposes wrongdoings, gathers significant information, instigates systemic change, and serves the public interest. She maintains that many of the highest achievements in journalism are the result of undercover reporting. Kroeger concludes that undercover reporting should be considered legitimate and honorable, as it fulfills the highest aims of journalism. Brooke Kroeger is a professor and the director of global and joint program studies at the Arthur L. Carter Journalism Institute at New York University. This viewpoint is adapted from her book Undercover Reporting: The Truth About Deception.

As you read, consider the following questions:

1. According to Kroeger, what did the *Washington Post's* series on Walter Reed Army Medical Center in 2007 reveal?

Brooke Kroeger, "Why Surreptitiousness Works," *Journal of Magazine & New Media Research* 13(1), Spring 2012. Copyright © 2012 by Brooke Kroeger. All rights reserved. Reproduced by permission.

2. How has successful undercover reporting impacted the careers of journalists and editors, according to Kroeger?

3. What tenets of journalism does undercover reporting speak to, in the author's opinion?

This is an argument for a restoration of honor and legitimacy to the discomfiting techniques of undercover reporting. Why? Because of the value of undercover reporting to so much of the journalism that has mattered in the past century and a half, and because so much of the journalism that matters relies on these methods anyway, at least in part. . . . Many great journalistic exposés of myriad types have benefitted from the use of subterfuge and deception in their efforts to expose wrongdoing, to extract significant information that is otherwise difficult or even impossible to obtain, or to create indelible, real-time descriptions of closed or hard-to-penetrate institutions or social situations that deserve the public's attention.

To explain why surreptitiousness works, consider this brief revisit to the major journalistic achievement of 2007, *The Washington Post*'s series exposing unacceptable conditions at Walter Reed Army Medical Center, by reporters Anne Hull and Dana Priest. Within a day after the series began, work crews were on-site upgrading the mold- and rodent-infested outpatient facilities. Within weeks, the hospital's commander, the secretary of the Army, and the Army's surgeon general had lost their jobs. Congress scheduled special field subcommittee hearings on-site at the hospital, inviting testimony from some of the reporters' named sources. Three blue-ribbon panels began investigating how wounded U.S. soldiers who had served their country so valiantly could be treated so badly under the Army's own watch.

Praise was nearly universal for the work of the two reporters and photographer Michel duCille, and it was no surprise to anyone the following year when they won the 2008 Pulitzer

Prize for Public Service. Leonard Downie, Jr., the newspaper's executive editor at the time, captured best the underlying meaning of their triumph at a time when economic and technological convulsions in the traditional delivery of news had put at risk the very survival of serious, intensively reported journalism, the kind that requires unique skill and training undergirded by large commitments of time and money. To the Pulitzer judges, Downie wrote, "At its core, truly great journalism is about righting wrongs and changing systems that are unfair or do not work." His reporters had done exactly that. The newspaper, indeed the whole profession, proudly—deservedly—celebrated the achievement. Priest and Hull had spent more than four months doing journalism in the public interest at its shining, steam-blasted best.

How They Did It

In the rush to extol the series and its impact, no one gave more than glancing notice to how the two reporters had managed to gain and maintain such unfettered access to a U.S. military institution, let alone a military hospital, over so many months. Only the sparest details of how-they-got-that-story trickled out in those early weeks, the period when interest in the project was keenest. To readers, Hull and Priest reported on method in a single sentence, as Downie, who opposes misrepresentation and undercover reporting, later similarly explained to the Pulitzer judges in his letter of nomination. He said their more than four months at Walter Reed was spent without official knowledge or permission. They declined to discuss method with the *Post*'s own media columnist or with a reporter for the *American Journalism Review*. At the gentle urging of a public radio interviewer, they gave up just a bit more. "I mean we didn't go through the Army for permission, nor did we go through Walter Reed," Hull said. "We went to the soldiers, removing that middle filter, because we wanted to hear what their lives were like, and we wanted to witness these problems firsthand, and that required lots of time with these people as they went through their days."

At about the same time, the *Post*'s ombudsman reported that "The two set out, mostly separately and never undercover, and did the kind of plain old gumshoe on-the-record reporting that often goes unrecognized in this high-tech age." She quoted Priest, saying of Army officials: "No one was really paying attention," which allowed the two reporters to stay "below the radar for as long as we did."

The ombudsman's framing of the enterprise as "never undercover" provoked no known counter at the time or thereafter. But was that really the case? Only a few bloggers, apparently indifferent to the U-word's burdensome implications, praised the *Post* with compound off-handed references to its "undercover reporting," "undercover investigation," or "undercover reporters," but that was about it.

Thirteen months after the series was published, at Harvard's Nieman Conference on Narrative Journalism and in interviews closer to the time of the Pulitzer announcement, Hull and Priest provided a fuller explanation of how they had so deliberately and effectively avoided detection until they were ready to reveal themselves to Walter Reed officials six days before the first story ran. It meant identifying themselves at the guard gates with their driver's licenses, as every ordinary visitor to the hospital does. It meant not announcing their *Post* affiliations or declaring their real intentions to anyone who might then be obliged to thwart their actual purpose. It meant avoiding unwelcome questions by playing on the common assumptions and expectations of officials who encountered them in the hospital environment. It meant constant vigilance and a series of stealth moves designed to help them blend in unremarkably with the surroundings, making themselves scarce whenever those who might question their presence or, worse, kick them out, appeared on the scene. It meant separating, so one could continue reporting in case the other got caught. It meant taking pains not to reveal their actual purpose to anyone who would be obliged to report them. It meant intentionally shedding such tools of the trade as cameras and reporters' notebooks so they would not raise unwelcome questions during routine bag searches. It meant imploring the trusted sources they developed during those four-plus months not to reveal what they had learned of the reporters' purpose or even to acknowledge the reporters personally should they meet up by chance on the hospital grounds. It meant helping their sources understand how to avoid inadvertently giving the reporters away, including careful coaching in "phraseology"—Hull's term—for themselves and for the soldiers, families, and hospital personnel whom they took into their confidence.

A Perfectly Legitimate Approach

Key for Hull and Priest and for their sources was to steer authorities away from asking the awkward questions to which truthful answers would be required under ethical and policy guidelines common to journalists, the military, and hospital personnel alike. Key also was to be free to "roam around the 110-acre facility at various hours of the day or night and talk to soldiers and Marines without the interference of Army public affairs." Undercover assignments often require this approach. Also key was the end goal: to be in a position to create the kind of impact in print that would force Walter Reed to respond to the urgent, repeated complaints from patients and their families that it had ignored for far too long.

The extraordinary potency of the series eliminated the need to further justify why the clandestine behavior had been necessary, but it came nonetheless a month after their first stories appeared—in the form of a Philadelphia parable. A local television crew, attempting to replicate the *Post's* successful work at a Veterans Administration hospital in Philadelphia, fell into the trap of exposure-too-soon that Hull and Priest had so carefully finessed. That crew was detained and fined, and had its cameras and film confiscated. On top of that, no story resulted, except an embarrassing one about the crew's arrest for staging what local media reports described as "an unknown undercover investigation." More to the point, there were no meaningful results to show for the botched effort.

It is a fact that Priest and Hull met the minimum requirement and common understanding of most reporters, as contained implicitly or explicitly in every journalistic code of ethics. That is, the obligation to be upfront when confronted and never to tell an outright lie. And clearly, Priest and Hull at all times were prepared to identify themselves as reporters should the direct question ever be put to them. To their great relief, it was not. They entered a public place they had every right to enter. They identified themselves with a driver's license, like everyone else. Open to debate, however, and one of the issues explored in my forthcoming [book] *Undercover Reporting: The Truth About Deception*, is whether there is really a difference for a journalist between not ever telling a lie—emphasis on the word *telling*, because lies, to qualify as lies, are verbalized or written—and the deliberate projection of a false impression with the clear intention to mislead, to deceive. It is at least fair to say that in attempts to finesse their identities to authorities at Walter Reed, the human targets of their inquiry, those with the most to lose, Hull and Priest went as far from wearing a press badge as it is possible to get, short of posing as a patient or hospital staffer. Those points at the far end of the ethical continuum generally bear the label "undercover." Was their approach perfectly legitimate, even unavoidable, given the circumstances and the stakes? Especially in light of the results, most, I think, would argue yes. I certainly would. Did the use of these tactics undermine the value of the enterprise or call it into question? They did not.

On the Side of Angels

So why avoid the obvious term of art? Why distance the enterprise from the label, as if bringing attention to the undercover aspects of their efforts would sully the achievement? Sadly and unfairly, I believe, it is because the label "undercover" *would* have sullied the achievement, at least in the eyes of some important players. This is largely because of a movement against undercover reporting in some quarters since the late 1970s, a movement the *Post*—once a daring, open, and exemplary proponent of the practice—helped to instigate.

What also emerges from the record is that over and over again, going undercover has proved to be an indispensable tool in the high-value, high-impact journalism of changing systems and righting wrongs. It has provided an enduring, magnetic, if sometimes tricky, narrative form that never ceases to fascinate, even when the execution fails to scale the high journalistic or literary walls. Colossal lapses and misfires aside—[*Undercover Reporting: The Truth About Deception*] addresses these, too, and they happen relatively rarely—undercover reporting has also been at the forefront of important published and broadcast efforts to create awareness, to correct widespread misconceptions, to provoke outrage, and to give a human face—whether that face inspires horror or compassion or a little of both—to any number of institutions and social worlds that otherwise would be ignored, misunderstood, or misrepresented for lack of open access.

Even the most cursory review of the reporting that has proudly worn the undercover banner bears witness to this fact. In addition to its public service, the very best work in this genre also has aggrandized journalistic legends at the institutional level, lionized great editors, who are so essential to the guiding and crafting of these projects, and catapulted individual reporters to enviable careers. Prizes for projects that involved undercover tactics are plentiful and not just in the distant past. Like almost no other reportorial approach, setting out deliberately to fool some of the people at least some of the time has repeatedly produced important, compelling, and—this might be the key to the method's enduring popularity—often riveting results.

Most important, surreptitiousness in reporting is also, often, on the side of the angels. At its best, it speaks directly to eight if not all ten essential journalistic tenets pinpointed by Bill Kovach and Tom Rosenstiel in their book *The Elements of Journalism: What Newspeople Should Know and the Public Should Expect*: the pursuit of truth, loyalty to citizens, the obligation to verify, the independent monitoring of power, providing a forum for public outcry, maintaining independence from those journalists report about, the opportunity to exercise personal conscience, and—perhaps most pertinently—the ability to make the significant interesting and relevant.

| "Journalism ethicists have long been wary of deceptive undercover tactics . . . and with good reason."

The Ethics of Undercover Journalism

Greg Marx

In the following viewpoint, Greg Marx contends that undercover journalism is unjustifiable in most cases. He maintains that journalists who use sting operations and subterfuge to get a story can erode the public trust's in news agencies and undermine the professional integrity of investigative journalists. He concludes that undercover reporting can be a powerful tool and that it should be used with caution. Greg Marx is a staff writer for the Columbia Journalism Review *(CJR).*

As you read, consider the following questions:

1. According to Marx, when should undercover reporting be used?

2. What is the "ready-made complaint" against undercover reporting, according to the author?

3. What guidelines does Marx offer for going undercover?

When news broke in late January that James O'Keefe and three other men, two of whom were costumed as telephone repairmen, had been arrested by federal authorities and charged with "interfering" with the phone system at the New Orleans office of Sen. Mary Landrieu, observers of all sorts shared a similar response: What were they thinking?

Thanks to a statement O'Keefe has posted at Andrew Breitbart's BigGovernment.com and an interview he gave Monday night to Fox News's Sean Hannity, we now have a pretty good answer to that question. Landrieu had drawn the ire of some conservatives for her participation in a deal that helped advance health care reform, and the anger had grown amid claims that her office was avoiding calls from constituents. O'Keefe told Hannity:

> We wanted to get to the bottom of the claim that [Landrieu] was not answering her phones, her phones were jammed. We wanted to find out why her constituents couldn't get through to her. We wanted to verify the reports.

And while O'Keefe has acknowledged that, "on reflection, I could have used a different approach to this investigation," he also told Hannity he was operating in an established tradition: "We used the same tactics that investigative journalists have been using. In all the videos I do, I pose as something I'm not to try to get to the bottom of the truth." During the interview, he and Hannity name-checked a few specific predecessors, among them *PrimeTime Live*'s Food Lion investigation, *60 Minutes*, *20/20*, and *Dateline NBC*, including its *To Catch a Predator* series.

Considering the extent to which O'Keefe's activities are driven by political goals, it's debatable whether or not he really belongs to this family tree. But even taking him at his word, lumping O'Keefe in with those programs doesn't necessarily put him on the safe ground he's looking for. Journalism ethicists have long been wary of deceptive undercover tactics that those programs (and others) use—and with good reason. Overreliance on sting operations and subterfuge can weaken the public's trust in the media and compromise journalists' claim to be truth-tellers. Undercover reporting can be a powerful tool, but it's one to be used cautiously: against only the most important targets, and even then only when accompanied by solid traditional reporting.

The field's squeamishness with "lying to get the truth," as the headline of a 2007 *American Journalism Review* article put it, is well-documented. In the 1970s, the *Chicago Sun-Times* set up an elaborate sting operation at the Mirage Tavern to document routine corruption in city agencies; the sting worked, but the paper's Pulitzer hopes were dashed, reportedly because Ben Bradlee and Eugene Patterson disapproved of its methods. *PrimeTime Live*'s decision to have producers falsify résumés and smuggle hidden cameras into a Food Lion grocery store sparked contentious litigation (an initial $5.5 million jury verdict against ABC was reduced on appeal to $2). and drew two articles in CJR.

Most recently, Ken Silverstein, the acclaimed Washington editor of *Harper's*, posed as a foreign businessman to expose lobbyists' willingness to represent unsavory clients. Silverstein came back with a gripping story and had plenty of defenders, but institutions like the Center for Public Integrity sided with *The Washington Post*'s Howard Kurtz in criticizing his methods.

In other words, press criticism of O'Keefe may reflect ideological disagreement in some cases. More broadly, it no doubt reflects some *schadenfreude* from an institution he and his patron Breitbart have conspicuously disdained. But it's also consistent with the wariness with which much of the media—especially the print media—has long viewed undercover reporting.

There are practical reasons for that wariness. As other observers have noted, while the use of deception in reporting

Going Undercover Changes the Story

There is an additional risk when you are investigating an illegal trade and posing as a buyer or seller, in other words as an *agent provocateur*. Apart from the dubious morality of that, you also become part or the story and so change it. This, to me, means that you have already passed beyond anything recognisable as journalism. The most flagrant case of this was in 1994 when stories began to emerge of weapons-grade plutonium being offered for sale on the German black market. A number of reporters thought they would make a name for themselves by probing this trade. Some posed as sellers, others as buyers with unlimited money. As if this was not bad enough, some journalists working undercover as "buyers" then ran into others impersonating sellers. None discovered the true identity of the other and so their published stories were not of the "trade in death" as they claimed, but of two over-enthusiastic journalists fooling each other—and themselves.

David Randall, The Universal Journalist, *2000.*

can yield sensational results, it also lends the subject a weapon to wield against the journalist. The ready-made complaint: If the reporter has forfeited the high ground of transparency and honesty, how can his conclusions be trusted by the public? The fallout may not be limited to the case at hand. During the Food Lion controversy, Marvin Kalb of Harvard's Shorenstein Center worried that widespread use of deception "demeans journalism and damages badly the journalist and the public." (This is not a theoretical problem. In announcing the verdict in the Food Lion case, the jury foreman told ABC, "You didn't have boundaries when you started this investigation. . . . You kept pushing on the edges and pushing on the edges. . . . It was too extensive and fraudulent.")

To mitigate this concern, undercover reporters are urged to take care to situate what they've gleaned through deception in a structure of traditional reporting—to show that, unlike, say, *Punk'd* or *Candid Camera* or even *To Catch a Predator*, the gimmick is not all there is. Wherever one comes down on Silverstein's work, one of the more effective criticisms of it was that his original story never gave the lobbying firms he targeted an opportunity to comment. A similar criticism applies to O'Keefe's ACORN videos, which made him a national figure—whatever malfeasance he may have uncovered at ACORN, his failure to present his videos in any broader reportorial context made it difficult for the national media to take his allegations seriously. (And when other journalists did look into the story, they found that the footage, while containing some truly troubling material, should not all be taken at face value.)

That's not the only guideline for going undercover. While there are, appropriately, no hard-and-fast rules or central authorities for journalism, a checklist drawn up by Poynter's Bob Steele in 1995 is often cited for guidance on this issue. A few points on the list are probably too vague to be of much use, but the first two are valuable. They state that deception and hidden cameras may be appropriate:

When the information obtained is of profound importance. It must be of vital public interest, such as revealing great "system failure" at the top levels, or it must prevent profound harm to individuals.

When all other alternatives for obtaining the same information have been exhausted.

Whether something is of "profound importance" is obviously a matter of news judgment, but there's good reason to question O'Keefe's. If his focus on ACORN was the product of a worldview that vastly exaggerated that group's practical political importance, his decision that Landrieu's phone system merited a hidden-camera investigation was even more off the mark.

Public officials should be responsive to their constituents, and when credible concerns are raised that they aren't, the press should check them out. (In fact . . . reporters in Louisiana *did* look into those allegations, and managed to do so without resorting to costumes or cell phone cameras.) But even if O'Keefe's suspicions about Landrieu turned out to be true, her actions would count as little more than a good-government misdemeanor. Deciding that they warranted undercover treatment is a reflection of editorial judgment unconstrained by common sense.

Of course, O'Keefe's comment to Hannity—"In all the videos I do, I pose as something I'm not"—suggests that he skipped this balancing test entirely. Attempts to reach O'Keefe for comment were unsuccessful, but in an interview late Wednesday night Breitbart defended his approach. "My tactics are unorthodox, and his tactics are unorthodox, because the mainstream media is full of shit," he said. "When we report the truth, you ignore it." Later, he added, "You guys are creating the market for creative journalism—it wouldn't be there if you guys did your job." (Whatever the merits of this argument, it is not exactly the defense that O'Keefe has advanced.)

All this may seem like so much legalistic hair-splitting to readers and viewers; in the big picture, whether O'Keefe's work is best thought of as "journalism," "activism," or something else may be a niche concern. But as long as he's trying to claim the mantle of undercover reporting, it's worth noting that that tradition is more complicated, and more contested, than he's acknowledging.

> *"Every act of plagiarism betrays the public's trust, violates the creator of the original material and diminishes the offender, our craft and our industry."*

Telling the Truth and Nothing But: Defining the Problem

National Summit to Fight Plagiarism & Fabrication

The authors of the following viewpoint maintain that plagiarism—appropriating the work of others without attribution—is a persistent transgression in journalism, whether in print, broadcasting, or online news. The authors contend that plagiarism is unfair to the creators of original content, harms journalism as a practice and industry, and breaches the trust of audiences. They conclude that the solution to the problem is attribution and that strict standards must be upheld and endorsed across all types of media. The authors of this viewpoint compose a task force of twenty-three journalism, publishing, and higher-education professionals that formed to study how to define, prevent, and deal with plagiarism. Led by the assistant managing editor of the Los Angeles Times, *the executive editor of the* State Journal-Register *(Springfield, IL), and a professor from the School of Journalism at the University of Arizona, the task force produced the report*

"2: Defining the Problem," *Telling the Truth and Nothing But*, 2012, American Copy Editors Society, 2013, pp. 5–15. Copyright © 2013 by American Copy Editors. All rights reserved. Reproduced by permission.

Telling the Truth and Nothing But *and presented its conclusions at the National Summit to Fight Plagiarism & Fabrication, a part of the 2013 annual American Copy Editors Society conference in St. Louis, Missouri. The following viewpoint is excerpted from the task force's report.*

As you read, consider the following questions:

1. According to the authors, what is their position on handling the intent behind plagiarism?

2. Why are quotation marks in attribution only part of the answer, according to the National Summit authors?

3. How do the authors respond to the issue of self-plagiarizing?

Plagiarism is presenting someone else's language or work as your own. Whether it is deliberate or the result of carelessness, such appropriation should be considered unacceptable because it hides the sources of information from the audience. Every act of plagiarism betrays the public's trust, violates the creator of the original material and diminishes the offender, our craft and our industry.

The best way to avoid plagiarism is to attribute information, a practice available in any medium. Credit should be given for information that is not common knowledge: facts, theories, opinions, statistics, photos, videos, graphics, drawings, quotations or original wording first produced by someone else.

Journalists must know how legal concepts such as copyright, fair use and trademarks apply to the profession. But they must go beyond minimum legal requirements to serve the public interest and treat creators fairly. Although one cannot legally protect an idea—only its specific expression in a tangible medium is subject to copyright protection—journalists should attribute the original, distinctive or seminal ideas of others when the ideas form a substantial basis for their own work.

With all of this in mind, we affirm a golden rule of attribution: Principled professionals credit the work of others, treating others as they would like to be treated themselves.

We believe that principled news organizations develop and enforce internal standards regarding plagiarism, attribution and fabrication. They make clear to their staffs that transgressions are unacceptable. They nurture a culture of truth-telling by spelling out the rules; by providing mandatory and continual training to prevent infractions; and by dealing with transgressions forthrightly, firmly and fairly. The results are accuracy, honesty, transparency, informed audiences and better journalism.

Journalism itself is founded on the public's right to know about our wider society, its institutions and its leaders. To extend this idea, the public that consumes our journalism has a right to know how we do our work, where we gathered our information, how we know what we know; that we are telling them, to the best of our ability, the whole truth and nothing but.

The Solution: Attribution

In attempting to define plagiarism, we started with the presumption that we would have to couple the problem to the solution: attribution. In doing so, we drew upon the research of Norman Lewis of the University of Florida, whose authoritative doctoral dissertation on newspaper plagiarism provided an intellectual guidepost, and on the editorial policies of numerous newsrooms and news associations. A close reading of our thoughts will therefore reveal echoes of the work of fellow journalists, notably those who crafted the standards in place at the *Seattle Times* and National Public Radio, among others, and the guidelines advocated by the Radio Television Digital News Association and other respected industry organizations.

As a group of professionals drawn from the print, broadcast and digital worlds, from newsrooms and classrooms, from individual organizations and industry associations, we decided at the outset that our definition must apply to any medium in which journalists work. After all, few news organizations these days produce only a single product. Newspapers and magazines publish websites and apps, attracting more readers digitally than they could ever reach in print. Broadcasters are similarly using new media to extend their already wide reach. Digital news sites employ video, audio and other tools, showing the way for more traditional media. All of this is linked by social media, which bring our readers, viewers, listeners and users more directly under our journalistic tent. As the industry continues its deep immersion in new media, crossing from platform to platform, it makes sense for journalists to carry their standards with them.

Although the tools of the trade differ by medium—and the means of proper attribution differ accordingly—we believe that it is essential to assert the same principled standards and approaches for operating on different platforms. We recognize that broadcasting presents special challenges because of long-held traditions, the hyper-competitive nature of the marketplace and the very real constraints of air time. We nevertheless challenge that vital segment of the industry to embrace a stronger standard for attribution.

While online news sites employ the familiar forms of text, images, audio and video mixed with reporting techniques available only in digital media, the ease with which material may be copied and the speed of innovation create their own tests of professional standards. We maintain that online, as in all other media, respect for the work of others through clear, appropriate attribution is the best method to uphold the principles we value.

Attribution is both a professional responsibility and a good business practice. Online readers, for example, have indicated that they find reporting containing links to be more authoritative. In an era when media institutions are suspect, heeding the ethic of transparency on all platforms reinforces the position of professional journalists as credible sources of information. Moreover, clear attribution may challenge journalists to do better and deeper work, help stem the rapid spread of error in breaking-news situations and cultivate collaboration while driving competition.

We broadened our definition of plagiarism to cover the realm of ideas, encouraging practitioners throughout the industry to more generously and forthrightly cite the seminal, distinctive work of others from whom they draw inspiration in creating their own original works.

An unavoidable complication in any discussion of plagiarism is intent. Was the plagiarism deliberate? Was it inadvertent? Any effort to define journalistic standards must, in our view, consider the recipients of the journalism, not just the producers. Plagiarism harms the creator of the original material, our craft, our industry—but just as crucially, it is a violation of the audience's trust. Whatever the motivation, the outcome is the same: Everyone suffers.

Intent—to the degree that it can be ascertained—should influence how an organization decides to handle transgressions by its journalists. . . . But it's time to reject an all-too-common defense—"I didn't mean it"—and to focus on education, training and the setting of clear standards. It's time to call plagiarism what it is. It's time to assert strong standards and campaign for their broad acceptance, time to recognize our industry's recent transgressions and reshape the future. There's no time like now.

Fabrication

Fabrication is often linked to plagiarism but in some ways is its opposite: Whereas plagiarism is using without attribution material produced by someone else and assumed to be factual, fabrication is making up material and publishing it in the guise of truth. Both are acts of deception. Both are wrong, but fabrication is especially egregious.

Journalists are committed to seeking and presenting the truth. Knowingly creating false material or deliberately altering reported material is therefore violating the most fundamental functions of journalism. Regardless of the platform, fabrication destroys the credibility of offending journalists, calling into question the validity of all their previous work.

Journalists should never create sources who don't exist or pretend to quote people they haven't interviewed. They should not pose as eyewitnesses in describing a scene or event they did not see firsthand. They should not alter a quotation to change its meaning or use an answer from one question as the response to another. Datelines should reflect where reporting was done and not suggest falsely that reporters were somewhere they were not.

Although some fine columnists of previous eras created imaginary personas as a literary device, the practice is never acceptable in a news article. Any attempt at re-enactment or character creation—including the creation of composite characters—must be clearly and completely explained to the audience before it is presented. Sources must occasionally be shielded for their protection, but pseudonyms should not be employed to identify them. A pseudonym amounts to a fabricated name and thus raises the question: What else in this story may be made up?

Images should not be edited or enhanced in a manner that would mislead the reader and convey an untruth. Photo illustrations should be clearly labeled as such. The code of ethics of the National Press Photographers Association instructs: "Editing should maintain the integrity of the photographic images' content and context. Do not manipulate images or add or alter sound in any way that can mislead viewers or misrepresent subjects."

To put it simply, a journalist should never lie to the audience or be a witting party to the lie of another.

Broadcasting: A Call to Action

All journalists would agree that taking someone else's work violates the principles that are the foundation of our industry and our organizations. But to what extent do broadcast journalists commit plagiarism when performing "rewrite"—taking copy from wire services, network feeds or their own newscasts and recasting it to produce a more conversational delivery, add facts from different sources or aid the reading style of a particular anchor?

Broadcast journalists traditionally view the work of their print and digital counterparts as avenues of opportunity. When the day dawns with its fresh reporting cycle, broadcast news desks everywhere begin to look for the next big story. What has happened overnight? What angle has been missed? What event may be coming up that fits the audience demographic? All of these questions are raised as news directors, managing editors and assignment managers aggressively explore metro and community newspapers, online news sites, even other broadcast reports. We recognize this as a common, accepted practice in broadcast journalism.

But monitoring other sources comes with distinct responsibilities. The broadcaster must not give the impression that a story that comes from print or another medium is a creation of its own, but must give credit in its broadcast to the original author.

In its code of ethics, the Radio Television Digital News Association prohibits plagiarism and cautions that professional electronic journalists should not "report anything known to be false; manipulate images or sounds in any way that is misleading; plagiarize or present images or sounds that are re-enacted without informing the public."

A specific broadcast assignment growing out of the active monitoring of other sources should not merely copy or mirror someone else's original creation. Whatever the inspiration for a story, it should still generally require checking with sources for new leads and using good sense in assembling the pieces of a puzzle, all with the goal of producing a fresh story that serves the audience.

To that end, we advocate these hard rules regarding broadcasting and plagiarism:

- The physical lifting and broadcasting of someone else's words, images, audio, video or other work is always plagiarism and is never ethical behavior.

- When broadcasting what print or other media are reporting, on-air credit is appropriate and links or written acknowledgment of original sources should be included in the online versions of broadcast pieces. But giving credit should not be construed as a free pass for the verbatim lifting of copy from those original stories.

- An exception to crediting stories from other news sources may exist for those distributed through network, syndication or wire service feeds that are contractually intended for use, either verbatim or for rewrite, without credit. For example, television and radio network-feed services are available to stations by paid subscription to use at will in newscasts without attribution to the network. Wire services contract with stations in the same fashion.

- Using coverage in other media as a jumping-off point, providing ideas for broadcasters' own original reporting, does not run afoul of plagiarism restrictions and does not demand the same level of credit as does repeating another's work in a way that does not advance the story.

The key to combating plagiarism in television and radio reporting is a determination to generate original stories, looking for second-day ledes to pieces that may have originated elsewhere and providing clear, complete attribution for work derived from other sources. In light of shrinking newsroom budgets, plagiarism may have to be redefined to take account of former competitors sharing resources and working together to tell stories that serve the public interest.

Print: More to Be Done

When Norman Lewis undertook his doctoral study of journalistic plagiarism he confined his research to daily newspapers and their decades-long record of malfeasance. When Craig Silverman challenged the news industry to address the twin plagues of plagiarism and fabrication he documented a "Summer of Sin," drawing much of his recent evidence from newspapers and magazines.

Clearly, even in print, with its hallowed traditions and stated aspirations to the highest standards, journalists must do a better job of attributing, crediting and documenting. They must adopt practices that serve the audience and fellow creators alike while providing a first defense against plagiarism.

Journalists might understandably start the conversation with a question: How much information—a word, a phrase, a sentence—can be copied without committing plagiarism? That's the wrong approach. It is more productive to look for reasons to attribute information more often, more clearly, more generously.

As Lewis' research has shown, most instances of plagiarism in print can be classified as "garden variety," the taking of someone else's work by verbatim copying and pasting. Proper attribution would prevent nearly all such cases. Over time, more attribution will lead to less plagiarism. With that in mind, we advocate the following best practices:

Punctuation, wording, placement. The guidelines on plagiarism of the Walter Cronkite School of Journalism and Mass Communication at Arizona State University offer clear, direct advice:

> "Quote and attribute: Use the exact words in quotation marks and include who said it or wrote it. Paraphrase and attribute: Use your own words, but still include who said it or wrote it."

Quotation marks are only part of the answer. Taking a quote from another publication without crediting the source is plagiarism, pure and simple. Similarly, using a quote from a press release without disclosing its source is misleading, suggesting that it came from an interview or that it is the first-hand knowledge of the reporter.

By the same token, vague references such as "reportedly," "sources said" and "according to authorities" are not enough. They do little to inform while giving journalists a false sense that they have fulfilled their obligation to the audience. Attribution should serve to answer questions, not raise them. (And journalists should not exaggerate; a single source is not "sources.")

Context and other narrative concerns will dictate where to place attribution and how often to use it. The goal in all instances should be to connect the information being cited and the underlying sources as closely and as clearly as possible, with the audience always in mind.

Using (and reusing) work by others. Many publications rely on wire services, syndicates and other outside providers. The *Los Angeles Times'* ethics guidelines offer succinct advice for handling such material: "We conduct our own reporting, but when we rely on the work of others, we credit them. When wire reports are used, we should clearly attribute the source in the narrative." The *Seattle Times* goes into greater detail, covering the melding of multiple wire services, bylining and crediting, and other everyday situations.

The practice of reusing previously published material raises an intriguing question: Can one self-plagiarize? Perhaps a better way to frame the discussion is to consider the term "recycling material without disclosure," as discussed in a Poynter Institute post about Jonah Lehrer's serial reuse in The *New Yorker* and *Wired* of material he had previously written for other publications. By any name, what Lehrer did was wrong: In no case should journalists copy material they have written for previous employers.

And by any name, the copying of one's prior work—either as an individual journalist or as a news organization—calls for common-sense precautions. On the one hand, the practice can be effective. An example is the reuse of previously vetted background language in a running news story that is being updated or followed up frequently over the course of a news cycle or many days. Such material generally would not require attribution.

On the other hand, the older the material the greater are the risks and thus the need for clear attribution: "as the *Journal* reported at the time of his conviction," for example, or "as she told the *Times* while serving her first term." Information from the archives may have become outdated or may have been wrong but never corrected publicly. Publication in the past does not absolve the current user of the need to cross-check facts, draw from multiple sources and otherwise take responsibility for getting things right.

Jonathan Bailey offers a simple credo at his website Plagiarism Today: "If attribution can be done, it should be done. It's not only the right thing to do, but the best for journalism in general." He makes a further commendable point: "Though there's no shame in using information from previous reports, journalists need to focus on what they can add to the news. By acknowledging what came before, the focus is put back on what's new."

Online: The Wild, Wild Web

Technology has enabled reporters to produce accurate and timely news online, often in creative ways without the inherent restrictions of other platforms. Technology has also made online plagiarism quick and easy. The lifting of others' work—including blatant copyright infringement, credited or not—is common. Work in other media has been lifted by websites, and the reporting of digital journalists has likewise been plagiarized, online and otherwise. Neither practice is acceptable.

Like broadcast organizations (and, indeed, most news outlets in any medium), online news organizations can find inspiration for follow-up reporting in the work of others. But online journalists must accept the same responsibilities as their broadcasting counterparts.

Unique to online journalism is the ease with which work can be copied and distributed. That has spawned the revival of aggregation and curation, techniques that flourished in newspapers of the Revolutionary era, in the broadsheets of the abolitionists and in such early newsmagazines as Luce's *Time*. Online aggregation is the reposting of another's work, generally wholesale through automatic scraping or parsing of an RSS feed, without additional reporting. Curation is the individual selection and posting of a portion of another's work, usually with added material.

While some copying of others' material may be considered "fair use," journalists working online should take special care to ensure that they do not infringe another's copyright. Automatic aggregation, even with attribution, should never cross the boundaries of fair use and professional respect. The reproduction of inappropriately large portions of text may discourage a reader from visiting the original work.

Curated work should also be clearly attributed. Curators should strive to go beyond merely reposting another's work, possibly including references to multiple news sources or original reporting, context or commentary.

The advent of user-generated content and work posted by others on social media raises additional issues that can best be met by attribution and respect for copyright. The challenges in verifying such content make transparency in sourcing necessary—not just ethically but practically. Not all crowd-sourced material is credible, but its use by professional journalists implies that it is based in the truth.

Questions of copyright and fair use aside, it is always good practice to identify the work's creator in the clearest possible manner. The use of platform credit alone does not suffice—for example, sourcing a video clip to YouTube rather than the poster is akin to sourcing a print news story to the press that reproduced it.

Some platforms create further challenges to attribution. On Twitter, for example, another's authorship can be indicated through the use of RT and MT ("retweet" and "modified tweet") with an @ link to the creator's profile. Other social media sites have similar methods or tools to assist with attribution, such as the "via" sharing option on Facebook.

Indeed, the practices of social media offer lessons in how journalists can do a better job of attribution regardless of medium or technology. If a tweet pecked out on a cellphone can convey proper attribution through an RT, an @ citation and a hyperlink in only 140 characters, there is no excuse for journalists operating with greater freedom in print, online or broadcasting. The simple words "As reported by . . ." can go a long way.

| *"This may be a Golden Age of non-facts,*
| *the Era of Error."*

Errors Are a Serious Problem in Journalism

Paul Farhi

In the following viewpoint, Paul Farhi argues that journalism is plagued by errors and inaccuracies, from minor mistakes, such as misspellings and incorrect ages, to major mistakes, such as distorted quotes and omissions of important information. According to Farhi, one of the largest journalistic studies ever conducted indicated that journalism errors are currently (as of 2013) at their highest level since such research began. Farhi contends that such errors damage the credibility of journalists and news agencies, the public's trust in the press, and even how history and current events are understood. Paul Farhi is a reporter for the Washington Post *newspaper and a senior contributing writer for the* American Journalism Review.

As you read, consider the following questions:

1. What does Farhi say that inaccuracy in the media accounts for?

2. How do errors affect the sources used by newspapers, according to the author?

3. What evidence does Fahri provide to support his claim that corrections can be difficult to make in journalism?

In journalism, as in real life, stuff happens. It happened to Ben Smith on March 22, 2007. That morning, Smith, then a crack reporter and blogger at [the online magazine] *Politico*, got a dynamite tip: John Edwards, the 2004 Democratic vice presidential nominee, would be announcing the suspension of his campaign for the 2008 presidential nomination at a press conference that afternoon. The decision, Smith's source said, was precipitated by his wife's health. Elizabeth Edwards' cancer had recurred.

Smith knew and trusted his source; as he wrote later, the source spoke with "authority and detail" about Elizabeth Edwards' condition. But just one source? With Edwards' press conference mere hours away, Smith consulted his editors. Go with it, they decided.

Politico, just two months old, put Smith's story on its home page under a bold, declarative headline: "Edwards to Suspend Campaign." The scoop predictably lit up the media landscape. The [website the] Drudge Report headlined it with a siren. Smith did three radio interviews. TV stories followed.

Many reporters know the weightless, slightly sickening feeling of what came next. It's like the moment when the cartoon character, having run full throttle off the edge of the cliff into midair, realizes he is about to plummet to the canyon floor.

At the ensuing press conference, Edwards indeed announced that his wife's cancer had returned. But he also said her condition wasn't sufficiently dire to suspend his campaign. Contrary to Smith's story, he was staying in. "It was a really awful moment, personally," recalls Smith, who went on to become editor of [the website] BuzzFeed. Reflecting on his mistake, he adds, "As with so many moments in reporting, I don't take a single clear lesson from this. But credibility is the coin of the realm, and I could feel the hit mine took with this."

He's right about being wrong, of course. In a perfect world, we'd all report with unerring accuracy, quote with symphonic fidelity and write with the grammar, syntax and spelling of an Oxford English lit professor. But it doesn't work like that. Mistakes happen—and they hurt not just an individual reporter and his or her publication but the media's reputation as a whole. Read on; I speak from experience.

The Era of Error

Public trust in the news media has been falling for decades, and inaccuracies—perceived or otherwise—are a big part of the reason. Just 25 percent of those surveyed by the Pew Research Center last year [2012] said news organizations generally get their facts straight; 66 percent said stories are "often inaccurate." Only four years earlier, 39 percent viewed the media as mostly accurate; 53 percent said the opposite.

Mistakes have been a part of journalism since long before "Dewey Defeats Truman" [a famous newspaper headline prematurely and incorrectly declaring the results of the 1948 presidential election]. But even with better and faster tools to check information, it's hard to argue that accuracy is improving. Deadline pressure in the era of the 24/7 news cycle is relentless, and many reporting staffs are smaller than in the past. Plus, there are fewer safety nets—editors and copy editors—to catch reporters when they misstep. News organizations are keen to fact-check the statements of politicians, but they might consider putting their own houses in better order as well.

In fact, this may be a Golden Age of non-facts, the Era of Error. In one of the largest and most comprehensive studies of journalistic inaccuracy, academics Scott Maier and Philip Meyer found that reporting errors were at their highest level in the 70 years such research has been conducted. Maier and

Meyer went right to the source, or rather the sources, to draw this conclusion. They asked some 4,800 sources cited in 400 stories carried by 14 newspapers whether the stories about them were accurate. Answer: Not very often. The sources reported errors in 61 percent of news and feature stories, the highest defect rate since studies of this kind began in the 1930s.

The reported inaccuracies included the relatively trivial and objective kind—misspellings, incorrect ages, titles and dates, etc.—to the more profound and subjective, such as misleading or distorted quotes, the omission of information or the overplaying of inconsequential facts (read: hype). Maier and Meyer went further, asking the sources for their perception of the stories and the newspapers' credibility. Unsurprisingly, the ratings of both declined as the number and severity of errors rose. What's more, the greater the error rate, the less likely sources said they were willing to cooperate with the newspaper again. In other words, errors not only hurt the newspaper's reputation, they damaged the media's working relationship with the very people they cover.

The even worse news about this bad news is that the research was conducted in 2002 and 2003, with the results published in 2005. While the researchers haven't revisited the topic since then, there isn't much reason to be hopeful, says Maier, a former reporter who is an associate professor of journalism at the University of Oregon. Today, reporters are busy tweeting and blogging and sometimes shooting video in addition to reporting stories. "Reporters are doing more than ever before, and editors are asked to do more, too," Maier says. Journalists "just don't have the same scrutiny and time. It's not surprising that you see errors creeping into copy more and more."

Speed Kills Journalistic Accuracy

It's not hard to find a journalist who, like Ben Smith, has made an error that has been seared into his or her consciousness. Sometimes the snapshots from journalism's vast Mistaken Nation are appalling, depressing or hilarious, and sometimes all three at once. Joel Achenbach, a veteran *Washington Post* writer, once wrote a feature story for the newspaper about the National Spelling Bee in which he misspelled four words (the *Post*'s droll correction of the story said the paper "feels reasonably sure that the rest of the words in the story, or at least the vast majority of them, were correctly spelled"). Another time, Achenbach miscalculated the number of hours of daylight on the shortest day of the year. "I must have gotten 100 e-mails from people who were proud of their ability to add and subtract," he says.

Trip Gabriel of the *New York Times* recalls a threefer from a single campaign trail dispatch last year [2011]. His story misspelled [the late televangelist] Tammy Faye Bakker's last name ("Baker"), misspelled [former US secretary of state] Hillary Clinton's first name ("Hilary") and reported the wrong call letters for a TV station. "I should have done better," says Gabriel, "especially since I later wrote a piece about [Rep. Michele] Bachmann's penchant for playing fast and loose with facts," most infamously with her assertion that a vaccine could cause mental retardation. Comments Gabriel: "Count me as one of those who believes that you lose a few atoms of reader trust, individually and collectively as the *Times*, whenever you get even the small stuff like names wrong."

With all-the-time deadlines and a win-the-traffic scoop culture, speed kills, or at least injures, journalistic accuracy. CNN's and Fox News' race to call the U.S. Supreme Court's decision on health care reform in June led to headline-making gaffes.

Premature—that is, erroneous—news reports about the deaths of well-known people are practically a subcategory of their own, echoing [American author and humorist] Mark Twain's long-ago quip about the stories of his own demise [being an exaggeration]. Media outlets in the Detroit area reported the death of famed boxing trainer Emanuel Steward in late October [2012]; Steward was ailing, but was, in fact, alive at the time. The "news" that disgraced Penn State football coach Joe Paterno had died traveled far and wide in January [2012] at least half a day before it was true. The most notorious of these false reports may have been the "death" of then-Arizona Rep. Gabrielle Giffords in a mass shooting in Tucson [Arizona] in early 2011. As Craig Silverman documented on his *Regret the Error* blog, NPR [National Public Radio] was the first to report incorrectly on Giffords' death, followed by Reuters, CNN, Fox News, *The Huffington Post*, the *New York Times* and PBS' *NewsHour*.

Breaking news, naturally, is the kind most susceptible to being misreported. And thanks to the Web and Twitter, everyone can see news being reported, sometimes badly, in real time. The "fact" that the New York Stock Exchange had been flooded by Hurricane Sandy in late October [2012] was retweeted hundreds of times, including by many news organizations. The tweet rolled from Twitter feed to Twitter feed like an onrushing snowball, each time gaining credibility based on the say-so of the previous tweeter. The problem: None of the retweeters had checked the original source of the story. If they had, they would have learned that the story was a fabrication, one of several launched during the storm by a malicious individual who went by the nom-de-Twitter [pseudonym] ComfortablySmug.

It pays to keep in mind what NPR's then-executive editor, Dick Meyer, wrote in a public apology for the Giffords mistake: "Already all of us at NPR News have been reminded of the challenges and professional responsibilities of reporting on fast-breaking news at a time and in an environment where information and misinformation move at light speed."

Correcting Errors

While traditional correction boxes haven't disappeared from newspapers, the Internet has revolutionized old notions of correcting mistakes, and not always in a good way. The ability to repost breaking material quickly means that there often are no acknowledgments of error in real time, just a succession of fixes.

In September [2012], for example, both the *Wall Street Journal* and the Associated Press [AP] initially reported that the mysterious figure behind the controversial "Innocence of Muslims" video was an Israeli named Sam Bacile, whose financial backers included about 100 American Jews. Within hours, both organizations filed updates that eventually revealed that "Bacile" was a pseudonym, that there was no Jewish involvement and that the key figures behind the video were Coptic Christians. None of these subsequent reports acknowledged that the initial stories had been inaccurate. That information appeared a day later when the *Journal* and the AP published brief, freestanding corrections.

There's little doubt that digital technology has revolutionized the traditional corrections box. Fixing an error, and noting the correction at the top or bottom of the story, are faster and easier to do than ever. Technology also permits corrections to be crowdsourced. Many eagle-eyed digital readers are quick to flag problems when they spot them. On Twitter, where much misinformation surfaces, debunking it has become a cottage industry. A number of news organizations, including my own, have "report corrections" buttons that make it painless for those readers to alert an editor. The days when reader phone calls were passed from desk to desk by indifferent news aides would seem to be over.

Even so, it's not clear that it's any easier to get a correction now than it was in the hot-type era. In a 2007 study of 10 daily newspapers, Maier found that journalists are as reluctant as ever to acknowledge they were wrong. News sources noticed lots of errors in the newspapers' stories, he found, but they rarely complained about them. When they did, the response was about the same as if they hadn't bothered. Of the

130 cases in which a source informed the newspaper about an alleged error, the newspapers ran a correction only four times.

Then there are the mistakes that are so large, so pervasive, they may not be noticed as mistakes at all until long afterward. Several newspapers, including my own, ran probing after-the-fact stories about how they covered, often mistakenly or misleadingly, the run-up to the war in Iraq in 2002 and early 2003. The pithiest "clarification" of all time may have been the 2004 mea culpa ["my fault"] by Kentucky's *Lexington Herald-Leader*: "It has come to the editor's attention that the *Herald-Leader* neglected to cover the civil rights movement. We regret the omission." . . .

Media Myths

The danger is that this first very rough draft of history can calcify into something like conventional wisdom. As it happens, some of the greatest myths perpetrated by the media are about the media itself. One popular notion is that CBS News anchorman Edward R. Murrow's famous "See It Now" broadcasts in the 1950s "brought down" Sen. Joe McCarthy, the communist-hunting demagogue. Another is that President Lyndon B. Johnson concluded that he could not win reelection after another legendary CBS anchorman, Walter Cronkite, declared in 1968 that the Vietnam War was "mired in stalemate." Still another is that the press, particularly [reporters] Bob Woodward and Carl Bernstein of the *Washington Post*, drove President Richard M. Nixon from office in 1974 with a relentless stream of revelations about the Watergate scandal [political espionage and subsequent cover-up by the Nixon administration].

These tales have been told so many times (often by journalists) that they seem true. But each is a case study in what satirist Stephen Colbert labeled "truthiness"—a statement having an emotional foundation or the ring of truth but with little or no evidence to support it. Each of these myths is dismantled in W. Joseph Campbell's 2010 book, *Getting It Wrong: Ten of the Greatest Misreported Stories in American Journalism*, which demonstrates the self-reinforcing power of mistakes.

Each media-driven myth, says Campbell, a professor at American University in Washington, D.C., shares a common DNA. "It has to be simple and plausible," he says. "It has to condense complicated events into a story that's easy to grasp." The stories involving Cronkite, Murrow and Watergate all share another trait as well: They cast journalists as the hero of the story, a self-flattering and perhaps irresistible narrative for reporters. . . .

Always Check It Out

Like every reporter, I've had my share of misreported names, dates and facts. Each error stings, but a sting doesn't last long. There's one mistake, however, that I'll never forget or ever stop regretting.

It started on August 13 with a tip from a man named Clyde Prestowitz. Hard on the heels of the news that CNN host and *Time* magazine Editor-at-Large Fareed Zakaria had been suspended for plagiarizing a *New Yorker* article, Prestowitz e-mailed me out of the blue. "I'd like to make you aware of a similar incident from my own personal experience," he wrote.

A similar incident? This sounded promising. I responded with interest via e-mail and spoke with Prestowitz several times on the phone. According to him, Zakaria had used without attribution material from Prestowitz's 2005 book, *Three Billion New Capitalists: The Great Shift of Wealth and Power to the East*. Prestowitz claimed that Zakaria had used a quote—from an interview Prestowitz had conducted with former Intel Corp. CEO Andy Grove—without citing its source in Zakaria's 2008 book, *The Post-American World*.

Prestowitz, an oft-quoted economist and former trade specialist in the [President Ronald] Reagan administration, sounded quite upset. But when I began to check his story, I found something that should have stopped me. In Amazon's "Look Inside" feature, which enables readers to browse portions of books online, I found that Zakaria had indeed noted Prestowitz's contribution in an endnote. It was tucked at the bottom of a note that first cited material from *New York Times* columnist and author Thomas Friedman.

Prestowitz waved me away. He said that credit appeared in version 2.0 of the book, which came out in 2011 (he was right about that; the footnote I read on Amazon was from the 2011 edition). He insisted that the credit had been added to the final edition after he and his agent had complained to Zakaria's publisher that earlier editions lacked the proper acknowledgment. The first edition and paperback (published in 2008 and 2009, respectively) didn't have the endnote, Prestowitz insisted.

At this point, I should have checked for myself. But a deadline loomed. I called Zakaria for his comment. He had a lot to say. But what he didn't say was most telling. First, he never denied not crediting Prestowitz (he said he couldn't remember). Then he launched into a justification of why not doing so was valid. "As I write explicitly [in the book], this is not an academic work where everything has to be acknowledged and footnoted," he told me. The book contains "hundreds" of comments and quotes that aren't attributed because doing so, in context, would "interrupt the flow for the reader," he said, adding that this was "standard practice" for authors such as Malcolm Gladwell, David Brooks, Friedman and himself.

My story went to press and appeared on washingtonpost.com that night. It began to pile up reader comments, mentions on Twitter and links from other news outlets. A success, I concluded.

Several months later, I can still remember that sickening, weightless feeling. I, too, had run off the cliff.

As became clear the next day, when Zakaria's publisher alerted my newspaper, my story was dead wrong. Zakaria had indeed credited Prestowitz in every edition of his book (a trip to the public library to get hard copies of each edition confirmed this). The *Post* not only corrected the story, it retracted it and added an apology to Zakaria.

In retrospect, I made not one but two mistakes. First, and most obviously, I should have independently checked Prestowitz's claim. Easy. The second part isn't so obvious. I shouldn't have taken Zakaria's non-denial of the allegation as confirmation of it, nor assumed that his attitude toward acknowledging his source material was a tacit admission of guilt.

Journalistic clichés often become clichés for good reasons—they codify ethical standards, stand as warnings of would-be pitfalls and reinforce the tribal wisdom. In my case, I forgot one of modern journalism's hoariest [oldest] clichés, one I won't forget again.

If your mother says she loves you, check it out.

Periodical and Internet Sources Bibliography

The following articles have been selected to supplement the diverse views presented in this chapter.

Rebecca Davis	"When Journalists Become Criminals," *Daily Maverick* (South Africa), August 12, 2013. www.dailymaverick.co.za.
Kelly McBride	"Journalism's Problem Is a Failure of Originality," *Globe and Mail* (Toronto), September 28, 2012.
Philip Meyer	"Tricks of the Trade," *Nieman Reports*, Winter 2013.
Richard Moore	"All Around America, It's the Myth of Objectivity," *Lakeland Times* (Minocqua, WI), March 30, 2012.
Nicholas Schmidle	"Smuggler, Forger, Writer, Spy," *The Atlantic*, October 4, 2010.
Craig Silverman	"Journalism's Summer of Sin Marked by Plagiarism, Fabrication, Obfuscation," Poynter, September 10, 2012. http://poynter.org.
Emily Esfahani Smith	"Ends vs. Means: The Ethics of Undercover Journalism," *The Blaze*, March 9, 2011.
Margaret Sullivan	"When Reporters Get Personal," *New York Times*, January 5, 2013.
Mallary Jean Tenore	"What Journalists Need to Know About Libelous Tweets," Poynter, August 8, 2011. http://poynter.org.
Edward Wasserman	"The Plagiarism Panic in Journalism," *Huffington Post, The Blog*, September 19, 2012. www.huffingtonpost.com.

OPPOSING
VIEWPOINTS®
SERIES

CHAPTER 2

How Should Journalism Be Practiced?

Chapter Preface

To ensure that information—from names and dates to quotes and sources—are correct and verified, news articles and reports are fact-checked. Agencies either have fact-checkers on staff or entire departments dedicated to the task, as getting it right the first time is paramount. "Documenting real events is serious. The most interesting pieces are often the most difficult to confirm, and when checkers are unable to speak directly to sources, much of the burden of verification falls on the author. This always involves some risk," writes veteran fact-checker Sarah Harrison Smith. Smith explains that mistakes can come at a hefty expense and chip away at journalistic integrity. "Fact checking can save publishers and writers from libel damages. More importantly, checking can save the press's reputation from being tainted by cynicism when readers become hardened to errors, both large and small,"[1] she writes.

In recent years more fact-checking websites, such as FactCheck.org and PolitiFact.com, have appeared to scrutinize what is published in the news media, particularly regarding politics and public policy. Some commentators suggest that the existence of these sites reflects poorly on the current performance of journalists, reporters, and new agencies. "Fact-checking sites offer an interesting insight into detailed political discourse, but it's hard to understand where the public benefit lies when rulings are nothing short of polemic discussion about 'truth' without proper journalistic framing," contends Bronwen Clune, vice-president of the Public Interest

---

1. Sarah Harrison Smith, *The Fact Checker's Bible: A Guide to Getting It Right.* New York: Anchor Books, 2004.

Journalism Foundation in Australia. "Journalists need to gain back this lost ground in their everyday reporting, not outsource it," she says.[2]

It is also argued that fact-checking websites can have a negative effect on reporting and the priorities of journalists. "The current expectation that fact-checks should be produced after every major political event—and that they should find falsehoods to expose—too often leads journalists to try to fit critiques of one-sided rhetoric into that template," explains Brendan Nyhan, a political scientist and media critic. He says that these sites attract attention away from major issues by continually emphasizing simple errors and flubs. "At the same time, the narrative-driven and character-based pathologies of political journalism can infect factchecking, producing an excessive focus on trivial issues and pedantic criticism when it fits a prevailing media storyline,"[3] he maintains. The authors in this chapter debate how journalism should be practiced.

2. Bronwen Clune, "Are Fact-Checking Sites a Symptom of the Media Not Doing Its Job?" *Guardian* (Manchester, UK), July 15, 2013.

3. Brendan Nyhan, "When Factcheckers Get Trigger Happy," *Columbia Journalism Review*, September 6, 2012. www.cjr.org/united_states_project/when_factcheckers_get _trigger-happy.php?page=all.

| *"Citizen advocacy or citizen journalism? Whatever one chooses to call it, the news got out—and had consequences."*

Citizen Journalism Is a Valid Alternative for News and Information

Eugene L. Meyer

In the following viewpoint, Eugene L. Meyer contends that citizen journalism—the publication or transmission of information by nonjournalists—serves as a valid alternative news source, particularly in countries suffering suppression of, or restrictions on, free speech. Meyer concludes that how citizen journalism should be supported and funded in conflict areas remains a debate. Eugene L. Meyer is a journalist, author, and the editor of B'nai B'rith Magazine, *a general-interest magazine serving the Jewish community.*

As you read, consider the following questions:

1. What statistics does Meyer cite for jailed Internet journalists and bloggers?

Eugene L. Meyer, "By the People: The Rise of Citizen Journalism," Center for International Media Assistance, December 16, 2010, pp. 8, 9, 13, 16–17, 25–2. Copyright © 2010 by National Endowment for Democracy. All rights reserved. Reproduced by permission.

2. According to the author, what does Bill Orme assert about the state of citizen journalism in Africa?

3. Where did citizen journalism begin, according to Meyer?

The term *citizen journalism* "doesn't mean very much," contends Ivan Sigal, executive director of Global Voices, which combines staff and unpaid volunteers to produce a website that is both aggregator and originator of content. "There are a lot of sloppy definitions and a lot of assumptions on where people are coming from, or whether or not citizen journalism is a good thing, and a lot of anecdotal sorting without much data-driven or cluster analytics together."

Definitions range widely across the spectrum. In Asia, writes Kathleen Reen, Internews vice-president for Asia, environment and new media, "I'm not sure that the more widely understood or shared definitions . . . reflect the U.S. perspective at all."

Eric Newton, the John S. and James L. Knight Foundation's vice-president overseeing its journalism program and a strong advocate for citizen journalism, likes to cite the experience of Deerfield, New Hampshire (population 3,678 in the 2000 census), in defining what citizen journalism is and can be.

Deerfield is "a small town without a paper, TV or radio station, a very, very modest civic website done by the town hall," he said. "Yet it's an educated community with Internet access. Friends of the Library five or six years ago were sitting around, bemoaning the fact that hardly anyone wanted to stand for local election. And in fact only a couple of the many races were contested. So they got a very small grant, through J-Lab at [American University], one of our grantees—$18,000 the first year, $7,000 the second year—to launch their volunteer [online] news and information platform, the *Deerfield Forum*. They found in each subsequent year that the voter turnout increased, the number wanting to stand for office increased, the number of contested offices increased."

Citizen Journalism's Effectiveness

All well and good in Deerfield, New Hampshire, and in other parts of the world that are free and democratic. However, Newton adds, in countries such as Cuba, Iran, and North Korea, "it is quite the opposite. A person could end up in jail, being chased by the law, and have to flee the country, because they engage in what we call citizen journalism in the United States.

"So, citizen journalism is going to be effective in some areas and not in others. Each community has its own microclimate. There are some things you can write about in some parts of Mexico and [in] other parts you'd be killed. We are very far behind in our understanding of the cultural microclimates and community microclimates and how they affect all kinds of news and info flows."

What, exactly, is citizen journalism? "I suppose it is any kind of information, publication, and diffusion of information done by people not trained as professionals, who haven't worked in established media," said James Breiner, director of the Digital Journalism Center in Guadalajara, Mexico. "I really don't know how to deal with that term. It's all over the landscape." And when do social media become outlets for citizen journalists? "I don't consider Facebook a news medium," said Breiner, "but it's certainly a communications medium. More and more, you are seeing Facebook being used as an outlet for news media and a way for non-traditional voices to be heard."

There is also this overriding question: Are citizen journalists, even in the best of circumstances, real journalists? David Simon, former *Baltimore Sun* journalist and writer and producer of *The Wire* and other successful cable television shows, thinks not. "You do not (in my city) run into bloggers or so-called 'citizen journalists' at City Hall, or in the court house hallways, or at the bars where police officers gather," he told a Senate hearing on the future of journalism in May 2009. "You don't see them consistently nurturing and then pressing sources. You don't see them holding institutions accountable on a daily basis. Why? Because high-end journalism is a profession. It requires daily full-time commitment by trained men and women who return to the same beats day in and day out."

But, of course, in totalitarian states or countries that place restrictions on the free flow of information, upholding such professional standards can be problematic. It may be little comfort—but it also may help shape our worldview—that more Internet journalists than those working in any other medium were jailed as of December 1, 2008, according to the Committee to Protect Journalists. In the December 2009 survey, 68—or half of journalists in jail—were bloggers, Web-based reporters and online editors—a numerical increase of 12 and a percentage jump of 5 points. . . .

Citizen Journalists Can Have an Impact

Yet, there are instances where citizen journalism in inhospitable places clearly has had a direct impact on the course of events. The question is whether such online activism is advocacy or straight journalism, and how much the distinction in such countries actually matters.

OhmyNews, launched on February 22, 2000, with the mantra "Every Citizen Is a Reporter," is widely credited with influencing the 2002 presidential election in South Korea. The citizen journalist website provided an alternative news source, and successful candidate Roh Moo-Hyuan benefitted from counter-arguments his supporters posted on *OhmyNews*.

In Mexico, through an Internet-generated campaign spurred by dissatisfaction with corruption in government, voters protested the July 2009 elections not by staying away from the polls but by making an "X" across their ballots. The "voto nulo" campaign came out of the blogosphere and videos posted on YouTube. It was a powerful use of the Internet to galvanize citizens into taking action. Not citizen journalism, precisely, but powerful nonetheless.

Underscoring the importance Mexicans place on access to the Web was "InternetNecesario," a movement to protest a 3 percent internet service provider tax proposed by the administration of President Felipe Calderón. After the movement generated 35,000 tweets from more than 7,000 Twitter participants and more than 8,300 members on Facebook, the Mexican Senate voted to overturn the tax in October 2009.

In Guatemala, also in 2009, Jean Anleu urged followers on Twitter to withdraw their money from banks associated with corrupt politicians. Anleu was identified and arrested on the grounds he was inciting the collapse of the economic system. Within hours, the online universe was ablaze with indignation, and funds were raised to bail him out.

"Something like that never would've happened without Twitter and Facebook," said James Breiner. "It used to be you could just arrest anybody and disappear them. Case closed, they're gone. You can't do that now. The great thing about citizen participation is you can publicize stuff that formerly wouldn't get publicized, and in a medium that is mass distributed." Social media are also credited with turning out 10,000 anti-government street protestors in Moldova in the spring of 2009.

Citizen advocacy or citizen journalism? Whatever one chooses to call it, the news got out—and had consequences. . . .

Starting from Scratch

As media development advisor in the United Nations Integrated Peacebuilding Office in the West African country of Sierra Leone, Bill Orme had a front row seat to watch citizen journalism at work in a troubled land.

"It's kind of remarkable," he said. "Here was this nation that had undergone a tragic, brutal horrific nearly dozen years of civil warfare with a huge number of casualties, followed by a large United Nations presence, 35,000 troops at the peak. Despite all those divisions, it has now had two sequential national elections, very hard-fought and very close, and the populace at large accepted the results immediately and without any question and challenge."

Orme attributes the peaceful elections directly to the role citizen journalists played via the medium of radio, which the UN instigated. "If it wasn't for that radio coverage, everyone agrees that wouldn't have been the case," he said.

"Radio is really the only medium" in Sierra Leone, he said. "TV exists in very rudimentary form in the capital city. The combined newspaper circulation in the country is 40,000 to 50,000, if that, divided between 15 or 20 papers, almost all in Freetown [the capital]," in a country with a population of 5.3 million in 2010.

Orme's office recruited volunteers to gather news to be broadcast. "Part of the strategy was to ensure that the actual vote count and processes all went according to international norms, and also that the public had a chance to follow the news in real time and believe in the credibility of the process. So all the independent radio stations created a joint national coverage network.

"Local reporters in most places weren't professionals. They were volunteers given training and tape recorders and cellphones and told how to cover elections. It's kind of remarkable."

Cellphones are used to text to radio stations, and they are "the revolutionary change, approaching 100 percent in Sierra Leone," Orme said. Texting is cheaper than voice calls, and it is anonymous. "You text, the radio station gets it; you can ID the phone number but not the person. In politically or ethnically charged situations, people feel freer to be more candid in their messages or questions they send to radio programs."

Journalism and Citizenship

If the current times enable everyone to inform, analyze, investigate, then the responsibility of the journalist is to still do all of those things, via publicizing representative democracy. If current technology allows public spaces where empathy, mobilization, and expression may exist outside the formula mainstream media organization, then it is the responsibility of media organizations to continue providing these opportunities because these opportunities are representative democracy. Of course any citizen may choose to publicize representative democracy; it is not a task exclusive to journalists. But for journalists, it is the ethical responsibility that marks and bounds their profession, just like doctors are bound by the ethical responsibility to not refuse care, lawyers by the confidentiality of client information, and academics marked by the obligation to share and pursue ideas. It is this ethical responsibility that does not separate journalists from citizens or citizen journalists, but rather, reconnects journalism and citizenship within the ethos of a democracy.

Zizi Papacharissi,
preface to Journalism and Citizenship:
New Agendas in Communication, *2009.*

Use of cellphones for citizen journalism is still in its infancy in Sierra Leone, he said. However, in much of Africa, cellphones and radios are "the two dominant media, overwhelmingly."

While much of the continent lacks newspapers and broadband, Africa is in some ways light years ahead of the more developed world. "You're really starting from scratch," he said. "They never had land line phones; cellphones are the first they ever had. They leapfrogged that old-fashioned technology. In some ways, they're more in the vanguard than we are, figuring out how to use these tools in very affordable, inclusive ways. If we're interested in where journalism is going globally, it's one of the more interesting laboratories." . . .

A Greater Bandwidth of Opportunity

Citizen journalism—or citizen media—didn't begin with the Internet, Facebook, and Twitter, or with the advent of cellphones. Even in societies ruled by authoritarian regimes, the word has historically gotten out, whether from the mimeograph machines run in basements by the French underground during World War II, or in self-published manuscripts replicated with carbon paper or photocopied in countries of the former Soviet bloc.

But thanks to technology, today's iteration offers a greater bandwidth of opportunity and the ability to reach more people with both news and views, despite governmental efforts at suppression. "Citizen journalism requires not just an environment where it is possible to use the Internet and get the word out but also where there are enough activists willing to try. There is no place where that is completely absent now," said Douglas Wake, first deputy director, Office for Democratic Institutions and Human Rights of the Organization for Security and Cooperation in Europe.

Based on the evidence, such a bold assertion seems correct. Questions arise, however, over matters of definition and standards.

"In many parts of Asia," said Internews's Reen, "citizen journalists are unencumbered by legacy media; initiatives start from scratch, and are often less concerned with traditional newsroom models or whether or not they are linked to newspapers, or TV or print. There's a good deal of leapfrogging of experience going on."

Said Elisa Tinsley, director of the Knight International Journalism Fellowships at ICFJ [International Center for Journalists], "Citizen journalism takes different forms in different places, depending on the attitudes of society. They can't be advocates, and therein should lie the difference between professional and citizen journalists. It's difficult to hold citizen journalists to the same standards without [their] understanding the rules and guidelines of professional journalism. I don't think it's easy to put a definition. It can be a very gray area."

It can be a gray area not only for media thinkers and implementers but also for funders, who have their own perspectives and agendas and are seeking to render assistance in a changing political and technological landscape. One threshold question: Should donors, including governments, support citizen journalism directly, or indirectly?

"It's fine to support infrastructure—to build up broadband networks, support legal environmental, education and training, digital media literacy," said Sigal of Global Voices. "But governments should stay away from directly funding individuals because it looks like they're buying them off, and they are."

Sigal believes funders need more data-driven research to justify their investments. "Funding governments have foreign policy and economic agendas; corporate funders, such as the Gates Foundation, see citizen journalism projects as a means to an end and insist on measurement," he said. . . .

Amra Tareen, of [the website] AllVoices, believes that donors "should not fund local, small things. People want to belong to something big. Small communities stay for a while but lose steam. All these people funding local citizen journalism need to get together. That's how this will become a big movement—or it won't." Aki Hashmi, AllVoices chief marketing manager, thinks that funders hoping to effect change "need a platform like AllVoices to enable the masses in parts of the world. They need this to power this type of movement."

Still, there is reluctance among funders to support citizen journalism in conflict areas, though some do, covertly. So much of the focus, at least in public, has been on citizen journalism success stories. Treading in more dangerous waters may be necessary.

"We are so intent on finding and celebrating successful citizen media projects that we might be blinding ourselves to the lessons we can learn from failures," Sigal said at the Global Voices Media Summit.

"I think a lot of the media training groups, the free press groups—when they are involved not just in a place like Burma but in the Balkans, in Central Asia, and a good swatch of Africa—understand that there is no way you can support an independent journalist without essentially working against the current government," said [Susan] Moeller [director of the University of Maryland's International Center for Media and the Public Agenda]. "In so many of these places, the [governments] are on record as trying to repress free and independent media. Is that advocacy, activism, objective journalism? Or at once all of the above?"

Such a question may not sharpen the focus on citizen journalism, but it necessarily widens the lens through which such efforts must be viewed.

| *"For all the benefits of citizen media,*
| *... it's been called untrustworthy,*
| *shoddy and inarticulate."*

Citizen Journalism Lacks Credibility

Chris Hogg

In the following viewpoint, Chris Hogg contends that citizen journalism—news and reports published or transmitted by non-journalists—lacks credibility in the eyes of professional journalists and editors. Two main concerns are that citizen journalists do not fully grasp the newsgathering process and that they are not held to the standards and principles of mainstream journalism. Hogg concludes that the future of journalism remains uncertain but that many people see a place for citizen journalism alongside traditional journalism. Chris Hogg is chief executive officer of Digital Journal, a global digital media network.

As you read, consider the following questions:

1. According to Hogg, what is one critical thing citizen journalists do not understand?

2. What does the author say about citizen journalists and false news?

3. Why are citizen journalists not yet being attacked for biased reporting, according to Hogg?

Citizen media is changing the face of journalism, but to what extent? Outlets like CNN, Fox and Canada's CTV have embraced user-generated news, and YouTube hopped on-board awhile ago. The *Washington Times* even devoted an entire section to articles by its citizen reporters.

The *Times'* executive editor John Solomon said, "We know there are many issues and communities we have not been able to fully cover within the confines of a newsroom budget, and we are excited to empower citizens within those communities to provide us news that will interest all our readers."

For all the benefits of citizen media, its critics point out the downsides of this rising trend. It's been called untrustworthy, shoddy and inarticulate. So how can citizen media gain the trust of both reporters and an ever-skeptical news audience? And how can it complement the mainstream media?

Citizen Journalists Are Amateurs

"I worry that many citizen journalists are basically amateurs who are simply mimicking what they see on TV or in the press, to varying degrees of success," says Jack Kapica, a former reporter for Canada's *Globe and Mail* and current writer and editorial advisor for DigitalJournal.com. "Much of the writing I've read, on most citizen journalism sites, shows little understanding of the process of gathering the news and writing it in a conventional form. Conventionality of presentation is important because it can give readers a recognizable framework to assess and understand what's being written."

Style issues aside, Kapica says citizen journalists need to focus on doing more original reporting rather than working as a rewrite desk in a newsroom. "One of the critical things many citizen journalism writers do not understand is the necessity of interviewing people and quoting them. The value of original quotes cannot be overstated. Too frequently I see citizen journalists quoting the mainstream media stories and I can't see how this differs from mainstream media."

Kapica believes citizen journalism, when done correctly, can be very powerful because of its speed and the ability of the fledgling industry to be anywhere at any time. That said, he also believes the world of citizen journalism needs to be encouraged to hold high standards of itself and practice sound journalistic principles.

Paul Knox, Chair of the School of Journalism at Ryerson University in Toronto, says trustworthy user-generated news has to be subject to the same quality-control mechanisms as mainstream journalism.

"Traditionally we put our trust into organizations who are set up to perform that trust, whether they're mainstream or alternative sources. It's more efficient to have that happening by a professional, by people who have had some knowledge on how to do it. We don't all wire our own houses, so we shouldn't all write our own news."

Knox said many mainstream journalists may be skeptical of citizen journalism, but emphasized that's what they are taught to do. "As reporters, we're trained to be skeptical, not to just take someone's word for it. We've also been trained to be on the lookout for people who are trying to convince [us] of things that aren't necessarily true. All of that is part of a reporter and editor's training. Like it or not, those things happen in our society."

Knox is critical of surveys that indicate how much people trust the mainstream press. "Someone who reads the *Globe and Mail* and says it's full of shit—that person doesn't immediately stop their lives and become a reporter," says Knox. "So why would they trust a citizen journalist any more? In the U.S. there have been some very high-profile cases where the mainstream media fell short of the standards they themselves set, but I don't think the broad brush criticism of the media has been fair."

In fact, citizen reports have been discovered to be phony. Remember the CNN iReport story last year [in 2008] about Apple's then-CEO, Steve Jobs, suffering a heart attack? It was reported to be breaking news but was later discovered to be false.

While studies show many people are increasingly skeptical of the mainstream press, some believe citizen journalists are guilty of the same thing.

"I see [citizen journalists] freely mixing opinion with factual reporting in obvious ignorance of how this is a conflict of ambition," Kapica says. "In one story I read a while ago, a fairly well-structured news story suddenly included the following sentence opener: 'Now come on, folks . . . ' If the mainstream media tried to pull a stunt like that, it would be flayed for bias. For some lucky reason citizen journalism is being held to a different standard."

Kapica believes it's only a matter of time until citizen journalism starts to field attacks for biased reporting. "If citizen journalism becomes mainstream, then it too will be criticized for not being trustworthy," he notes. "At the moment it's getting a free ride. It's axiomatic in journalism that the more influential you are, the more insults and the bigger lawsuits you attract. Since citizen journalism sites do not yet have a perceptible clout, they are spared criticism, leaving the impression they're 'better' if only because they're not attracting vitriol [bitter criticism]."

When it comes to trust of user-generated media, Kapica believes editing and supervision is necessary. "I know much of what I have written would have killed me had not a sharp-eyed editor spotted me saying something I didn't mean."

© Brainstuck.com.

The Future of Journalism

The future of journalism, and its business model, remains uncertain. Most people interviewed by DigitalJournal.com agree it will morph into some sort of hybrid journalism, blending the immediacy of social news sites like Twitter and Facebook with the accuracy and dependability of traditional journalism.

Kapica says newspapers that have created citizen journalism websites separate from their newspapers are on the right track, "as long as they nurture their writers and exercise oversight." He adds, "But they have to do it right; you can't create a newsroom from scratch and expect readers to flock to it overnight. You need reputation, and building a reputation

95

takes a lot of time, something the Twittering speed-freaks of online journalism have too little of."

Stephen Dohnberg, who works as both a "professional" and citizen journalist, says citizen journalists need to do a better job of practicing sound journalism. Self-training isn't easy, though. "Unless one has a big trust fund or a good amount of venture capital, it is hard for the average citizen journalist to know there are ethics and a methodology. It is incumbent on citizen journalists to distinguish themselves from bloggers and that means learning some of the basics. At the end of the day, the goal for honest reporters and journalists is the same: Presenting facts and information, not entertainment."

That said, he also admits the term "citizen journalism" is an Achilles' Heel to those who practice it; "It does a disservice to the people doing the really hard work and following the example of the best of reporting," he said. "At the same time, it lumps [in] veiled advocacy-based writing and self-interest blogs with agendas."

Dohnberg suggests public relations personnel should provide more access for citizen reporters. "In essence, they are reporters if they are doing the hard work involved," he says. "So why undermine oneself? And after all, is a journalist not a citizen? It almost intimates this hierarchy like the way [police] have taken to referring to fellow citizens as 'civilians.' Ridiculous."

Abby Goodrom, Velma Rogers Graham Research Chair at Ryerson University, believes citizen journalism is capable of being professional and can add value to a mainstream media report, but the world is just at a transitional point where it's figuring out what its future holds.

"The whole discourse gets positioned as two opposites fighting against the middle," she says. "In fact, I think there is a much broader spectrum here, but if we don't position it as us against them it doesn't make the news. I think we're actually seeing much more cooperation and collaboration."

Goodrom says newspapers and broadcasters wouldn't allow people to contribute if they didn't see the value in doing so. However, she's skeptical about how much traction citizen journalism can get in the industry because of funding.

"This notion that citizen journalism will replace the media is impossible because it can't afford to," she tells DigitalJournal .com in a phone interview. "At some point, if you had enough citizen journalists banded together, that becomes like a mainstream media."

| "Clearly, the journalism major is unnec-
essary for entry into the industry."

A Journalism Degree Is Unnecessary

Michael Tracey

In the following viewpoint, Michael Tracey challenges the purpose of a formal journalism education. He contends that a journalism degree is not required to obtain a job in journalism. He further maintains that the existence of a journalism degree discourages people with degrees in other fields from pursuing a career in journalism. Tracey concludes that the solution is to eliminate the journalism degree and integrate journalism education and training into other academic programs. Michael Tracey is a journalist based in Brooklyn, New York.

As you read, consider the following questions:

1. Why may the change in Northwestern University's journalism program have wide implications for journalism education across the United States, according to Tracey?

2. According to Tracey, what is Jay Rosen's observation about formal training and professional journalists?

3. What does the author say is behind the promotion of "new media integration" in Northwestern University's journalism curriculum?

Last fall [2010], by a vote of 38 to 5, faculty at Northwestern University's Medill School of Journalism approved a doozy of a name-change. The board of trustees then lent its final imprimatur [approval] in March, and with that, one of America's leading journalism schools was henceforth known as—take a deep breath—"The Medill School of Journalism, Media, Integrated Marketing Communications."

There's a lot to unpack here, but I'd first call your attention to the faculty's apparent rejection of Associated Press [AP]–sanctioned grammatical norms [in the school's new name]. Given the industry's longstanding reverence for the AP stylebook as a semi-divine standard of journalistic propriety, this has the makings of a landmark decision.

That aside, I've found that the most common reaction people had to the news was something along the lines of, "What the heck is Integrated Marketing Communications [IMC]?" Northwestern's website describes it as a "Medill-invented field," which partially explains the widespread confusion. But even so, there seems something deliberately obfuscatory [confusing] about the term; like it was "invented" in a boardroom by middle-aged white men desperately brainstorming ways to appear cutting-edge. Indeed, its function is ultimately reminiscent of those banal slogans often found in a college's promotional material, like "Commitment to Excellence" or "Where Leaders Look Forward."

An IMC "certificate" is available to Northwestern undergraduates who complete five credits of requisite coursework. The program, according to Medill's website, prepares students for entry-level positions in fields like advertising, public relations, and "corporate communications." Of course, there's nothing especially new or surprising about the actual curricula—business students are taught similar stuff, and PR [public relations]-training has been a feature of journalism departments for years. The real question is why one of the country's leading *journalism* schools has elected to so fully integrate *marketing* into its identity. You need not be a stuck-up purist to prefer that the two be kept safely apart. Moreover, I think it's fair to say that journalism and marketing are in fact profoundly antithetical enterprises.

As one would hope, the big name-change news was met with derision from just about everyone not associated with Medill. Mark Oppenheimer, director of the Yale Journalism Initiative, summed up the prevailing sentiment when he wrote "We should all be a little concerned that the same schools that teach people to see through bogus claims are also the same schools teaching students how to perpetuate bogus claims."

Jeff Jarvis, a Medill alumnus and noted professor of journalism at the City University of New York, directed a less-than-equanimous tweet at his alma mater, calling integrated marketing "the kind of bullshit jargon your teachers should be editing out." One of the few faculty who voted against the change, associate professor Doug Foster, told me the new name "fuzzes up the sense that this is an institution devoted, at its heart, to the essential values of journalistic practice."

One Man's Pedagogical Vision

The most pertinent question is whether the change can be taken as indicative of wider trends in journalism education, or if this is all just peculiar to Northwestern. Every institution has its eccentricities, and one must be wary of drawing broad conclusions about an entire academic field based on a single decision. But Medill's journalism program is widely heralded as one of the best around. It tops lists. It describes itself as "a jewel at one of the nation's elite universities." It has an impressive rolodex of notable alumni. So unless Medill's reputation has been criminally inflated, one can reasonably infer

Graduate Programs in Journalism Are Unnecessary

What about graduate programs in journalism? Unnecessary, I think. The best journalism graduate program is no journalism graduate program. At present the M.A. degrees are simply elongations of the bachelor's degree—with a long term paper (a thesis) thrown in. And there is no mental "hardness" to the degree. I cannot recall a single thing that I learned during my year-long journalism master's degree. I'm sure I got some instruction in something in my journalism courses, but I don't know what. However, I did some learning in the few "outside" courses (political science and history) that I took.

John C. Merrill and Ralph L. Lowenstein, Viva Journalism! The Triumph of Print in the Media Revolution, *2010.*

that what happens there has implications for journalism education in the rest of the country.

Most Northwestern people I spoke to agreed that the impending name-change is more symbolic than substantive, formalizing a cultural shift at the school that had already been underway since John Lavine, an entrepreneur and former movie company executive, began his term as dean in 2006. Lavine, who also teaches at Northwestern's Kellogg School of Business, declared his intention to "blow up" Medill's curriculum shortly after assuming office. According to the *Columbia Journalism Review*, his introductory manifesto contained "references, vague though they were, to narrowing the gap between the journalism and marketing sides of the school"—enough to make some faculty queasy from the outset. Lavine's clear assertion was that marketing and journalism are, in fact, complementary pursuits.

David Spett, a Medill alumnus who now directs the Center for American Progress's college journalism program, followed Lavine's tenure closely as an undergraduate. Three years ago, as a student columnist, Spett noticed something fishy about an article Lavine wrote for Medill's alumni magazine, in which the dean relayed high praise from several unidentified students for a new course entitled "Advertising: Building Brand Image." Spett suspected that stilted remarks like "I sure felt good about this class" were unlikely to have been uttered by a "Medill junior," and even if the quotes were perfectly authentic, he asked, what possible reason was there for Lavine to forego proper attribution? Everyone knows that allowing promiscuous anonymity is a violation of Journalism 101, and higher standards are surely expected of even the most unschooled freshmen. So Spett contacted every student enrolled in the course at the time, and sure enough, none corroborated the quotes. Lavine denied fabricating anything, but never provided exculpatory [freeing of blame] evidence—citing an email-related malfunction. An ad-hoc committee later cleared him of wrongdoing. The delicious irony, however, caused the school considerable embarrassment.

Ethical lapses notwithstanding, Lavine's pedagogical vision seems to have gradually materialized. Lindsey Kratochwill, a Medill journalism major and managing editor of the campus newsmagazine *North by Northwestern*, told me she's "felt that in some classes, there is sort of an emphasis on business, or how to 'market' your story." So goes Lavine's "narrow the gap" strategy: Insist that without attention to marketability, the journalistic enterprise is incomplete. My question, then: if this is the trajectory of the country's premier institution for journalism education, might it be time to reevaluate the premise of journalism education in the first place?

Unnecessary and Bad for the Craft

For the purpose of clarity, I'll keep this focused on the undergraduate journalism major, which seems to me can serve dual purposes: one, as preparation for students who wish to become professional journalists, and two, as an outlet for subjecting "the media" per se to academic analysis. The latter is certainly a worthwhile endeavor, perhaps best personified by Jay Rosen, the professor of journalism at NYU [New York University] known for incisively disassembling the hoary [old and honored] tendencies of mainstream press. But it's the former category—an academic program that supposedly prepares students to become journalists—that strikes me as conceptually dubious.

"Formal training in journalism isn't necessary," Rosen told me last fall [2010]. "It never has been. The percentage of professional journalists who attended J-school has never been more than 60. Compare that to law, medicine or accounting and it's clear that there are other ways to join this field than getting a degree in it. And that's the way it should be. Requiring a J-degree would be a regulation and we have an unregulated press in this country."

Clearly, the journalism major is unnecessary for entry into the industry. But I'd go a step further—on a whole, it's actually bad for the craft. Think about the social function of the journalism major. Overtly or not, it creates an implicit regulatory structure, endowing journalism students with the right to manage the university's newspaper by virtue of their participation in important seminars on media ethics and interview techniques. Conversely, non-journalism students are left with the impression that reporting is best reserved for those who've been formally trained to do it.

In reality, the opposite can be true: The most insightful kind of journalist tends to be one with proficiencies in other subjects. Oppenheimer, the Yale Journalism Initiative director, has it about right: "The animating belief of our program," he wrote last fall, "is that the best journalism training is expertise in the liberal arts—whether Chinese literature, chemistry, geology, or economics—along with the preparation to bring that expertise, in a tough-minded, hard-hitting way, to the media." So if you take a full major's worth of journalism classes, that's about twelve (or however many) less classes in the humanities that could've equipped you with an intellectual framework from which to approach your work.

The Objectivity Decree

Formalized journalism training also lends academic credibility to mainstream normative standards, the most notorious being the objectivity decree, which is still seriously entertained as a plausible ideal in journalism departments. To get a job in the "traditional" industry, one former journalism major told me, students are urged to maintain an image of unsullied impartiality, both personally and professionally. This means never taking part in public political events, never affiliating with any partisan organizations, never posting Facebook status updates that might indicate your opinions on matters of substance. Studiously avoid any demonstration of being invested in how the world works, lest you fail to meet the requirements for journalistic seriousness.

Of course, not all journalism students adhere to these dehumanizing rules. But among those who do, you have to assume that if they've managed to develop any kind of coherent world-view, it's likely to be terribly stunted. Not a big surprise, then, that their aspiration is to carry out the disengaged, consensus-affirming, status quo–reinforcing kind of journalism that critics like [controversial columnist] Glenn Greenwald have so mercilessly dissected. "The conventions of modern establishment journalism are designed to suppress any genuine adversarial challenges to political power," Greenwald told me recently. "In 2005, [the late Pulitzer Prize–winning journalist] David Halberstam said: 'By and large, the more famous you are, the less of a journalist you are.' I'd add: by and large, the more you cling to the orthodoxies of modern journalism, the less of a journalist you are."

Incorporate Journalism into Other Subjects

An irony here is that most journalism majors, simply on account of steadily decreasing employment opportunities, are not going to enter the field. Where do they tend to end up? "I have met approximately fifty journalism majors in Washington D.C.," says Timothy Carney, a columnist for the *Washington Examiner*. "And approximately four of them are journalists. I know approximately 250 journalists, and approximately four of them were journalism majors. My experience with journalism majors I meet—if they're in journalism at all—most of them are selling ads or something like that."

When [journalist] Michael Lewis famously skewered "the desperate futility of journalism instruction" in 1993, it was long before the internet upended the industry. "At journalism school," he wrote, "one does not simply report a story. One develops a 'search strategy for mass communication.'" Eighteen years later, such strategies can be developed with a meticulousness never before thinkable. Google now tracks every conceivable metric by which to gauge a story's popularity and profitability; search engine optimization and click counts have become an integral part of journalism's business model. So it's perhaps to be expected that someone like John Lavine would progressively infuse marketing into Medill's curriculum, under the guise of promoting "new media integration," because in his mind, he's throwing students a lifeline. In order to make those $40,000/year tuitions worthwhile, journalism students need to be prepared to take non-journalism work after graduation. And remember: Lavine's an accredited Future of Journalism expert, so he can authoritatively rationalize diluting the craft with academic-sounding bromides.

The Medill situation will only hasten the acceptance of a realization that everyone should already know: you really can't teach journalism. Therefore, you shouldn't be surprised when extraneous bunk like marketing becomes a prominent feature of journalism education. Once again, I have no doubt that there are many admirable journalists who were journalism majors, and I find the insights of journalism professors like Jay Rosen and Jeff Jarvis invaluable. But the contributions of certain exceptional individuals does not negate the overall social effect of journalism education, which is largely negative.

So what's the solution? My sense is that the aspect of journalism education most worth preserving is the hands-on experience with seasoned writers and editors. Instead of sequestering journalism into its own academic program, then, why not incorporate it into the teaching of other subjects? Bring in professional journalists who'll emphasize to students in the humanities and the sciences that they are just as entitled to "do journalism" as anyone else. And it's not nearly as complicated as they might think.

> "A good journalism education turns out students who think carefully and deeply."

A Journalism Degree Is Invaluable

Afi-Odelia Scruggs

In the following viewpoint, Afi-Odelia Scruggs defends the value of a formal journalism education. She maintains that it teaches students to search for answers, to ask fundamental questions, and to think. While she concedes that these skills can be learned on the job, she points out that employers are not in the business of teaching journalism and they are looking for candidates who already possess the skills necessary to do the work. Afi-Odelia Scruggs is a journalist and has taught journalism at both the high school and college levels.

As you read, consider the following questions:

1. What do critiques of journalism education overlook, according to Scruggs?

2. What is Scruggs's position on journalists' learning skills on the job?

3. According to the author, how should a journalism program be judged?

As fall semester 2012 moves toward mid-term, journalism education is gathering its defenses against assaults on its relevance.

Emory College announced last month [September 2012] that it is closing its program because journalism falls outside the school's emphasis on liberal education, according to Arts & Sciences College Dean Robin Forman.

"It's not our job, as a liberal arts college, to simply train people to be professional journalists—in the same way it's not our job to train people to be professional doctors or lawyers or businesspeople," Forman told a reporter from [the website] Creative Loafing.

He's not an outlier [someone on the fringe]. Bill Cotterell, a retired political reporter from Florida went even further. He compared journalism education to driver's education, where the real learning comes from "trial and error."

"Anyone who's smart can learn the 5 Ws [Who, What, Where, When, Why—the questions journalism programs teach students to ask and answer] in a couple weeks. And if they learn from their mistakes, they can get good at telling you what's really going on," Cotterell wrote on Tallahassee.com. . . .

These critiques and suggestions, however, focus on journalism's products—the stories filed, the photographs taken, the apps created, or the content aggregated—while overlooking the conceptualization involved in the process. After almost 25 years as a reporter, I'm convinced a good journalism education turns out students who think carefully and deeply.

That might sound strange, given my background. I didn't go to journalism school. Instead, I stumbled into the field in my 30s, after a few years as a freelance writer. I needed more than a couple weeks to learn the 5 Ws and 1 H ["how"], but a stint as a night cops reporter gave me some chops.

The Need for a Doctor of Journalism Degree

Just as law, medicine, dentistry, and other professions found it necessary to develop professional education on the graduate level, so also must journalism. . . . [No university] has yet established an independent professional college that offers, as law, medicine and other professions do, a professional doctoral degree, a Doctor of Journalism degree that would be on a par with a Doctor of Law, Doctor of Medicine, or Doctor of Dental Surgery degree.

Graduates of such a professional journalism school could more easily move to the top of their profession and achieve the prestige now held by medical doctors, lawyers, and dentists. They would probably merit better salaries than most journalists are now paid, thus leveraging upward the pay of all the other journalists, pay now so low—at least on the starting level—that many talented young people are deterred from entering the field.

Warren G. Bovée, Discovering Journalism, *1999.*

Along the way, I learned that powerful journalism springs from questioning and probing, skills I was taught as a liberal arts major. If I wanted a memorable article, I had to do more than get quotes from the school board meeting. I had to challenge assertions, perceptions and assumptions—including my own.

Otherwise, I wasn't a journalist. I was a stenographer.

Why Journalism Education Works

When I began to teach about 10 years ago [about 2002], I pledged to produce critical thinkers who could work as competent, committed journalists. I never assumed my students would go straight into the profession. (In fact, a former student became a rock musician before ending up at *Fortune* magazine.) And if they did, I didn't assume they'd stay in a single medium; in 2001, we were talking convergence. While I didn't skimp on mechanics, I knew my students could go wherever they wanted if they had a substantial intellect.

That's also the aim of a liberal education, according to the Association of American Colleges and Universities [AAC&U]. On its site, the AAC&U writes:

> "A liberal education helps students develop a sense of social responsibility, as well as *strong and transferable intellectual and practical skills* such as communication, analytical and problem-solving skills, and a *demonstrated ability* to apply knowledge and skills in *real-world settings*." (Emphasis mine)

I imagine Emory University agrees with that definition because the university belongs to the association. I just wish Forman and others—including some professional journalists—understood a good journalism education already accomplishes those goals in three important ways.

1. A good journalism education teaches students to search for answers.

Journalism calls the search "reporting." Other professions simply call it "research." The name doesn't matter as much as the expectation that students will develop the practice and carry it into their professional and personal lives.

[Journalism professor] Robert Hernandez communicates that expectation when he challenges his students to "Google it" instead of relying upon him for the answer.

"At first, they thought I didn't know the answers and I was using the search engine to cover up my shortcomings," he wrote for the Nieman Journalism Lab [website]. "But those who have truly embraced the Web know what that simple phrase really means: Empower yourself."

2. A good journalism education teaches students to ask the fundamental questions of all intellectual inquiry.

Journalists are so busy extolling the practical applications of the 5 Ws and 1 H, we forget how powerful they are. Adrian, [a commenter] at lifehack.org, explained the importance of the sequence in a 2007 post on New Year's resolutions. "All six questions are essential. Missing any of them leaves a gap that must be filled by assumptions or imagination," he wrote.

Any profession or field of study can teach students to employ the interrogative words. In journalism, however, they're inescapable. Habitual use of the 5 Ws and 1 H, paired with the push to discover answers, can result in the greatest benefit of a good journalism education.

3. A good journalism education develops intellectual curiosity.

Chalk it up to practice, the 10,000 hours of repetition necessary for mastery. After spending four years immersed in inquiry and investigation, curiosity becomes second nature.

Can a prospective journalist learn these skills on the job? Yes, but news outlets aren't in the teaching business. They're in the publication and sales businesses. They're in the delivering-content-to-an-audience business.

Like Bob Cohn, editor of Atlantic Digital [part of the *Atlantic Monthly* magazine], they're looking for folks who "have the right sensibilities—and the skills to succeed in this new age," not for folks who have to learn them.

A journalism program is a dedicated learning environment where students flourish or flounder. A good program should be judged by whether its students have learned to think, regardless of the field they enter or the jobs they eventually hold.

| "Journalism is a public service—not just another business."

Journalism Should Be Supported as a Public Service

Craig Aaron

In the following viewpoint, Craig Aaron contends that journalism is in decline and that it is an indispensable public service that should be saved. He recommends using nonprofit and low-profit ownership models to remove pressures from investors, offering incentives to collapsing media companies to sell their properties in the public interest, and establishing a journalism jobs program. Aaron further advocates for government-funded research and development for journalism and reforming the public broadcasting and media systems to emphasize community service. Craig Aaron is senior program director for Free Press, a nonprofit media advocacy group. This viewpoint is excerpted from a speech Aaron gave in 2009 at the Free Press Summit, a one-day multimedia event that focused on changing the media.

As you read, consider the following questions:

1. What data does Aaron cite to support his claim that newspapers remain profitable?

2. How does the author respond to the argument that the Internet is harming journalism?

3. What does Aaron call for in a government-seeded innovation fund for journalism?

When we talk about saving the news, first and foremost, let's be sure we're *actually making it better.*

At this point, it's hard to imagine things could be any worse.

By one count, 24,000 journalism jobs have been lost since 2008. Foreign, Washington and statehouse bureaus have been shuttered. Major news organizations are in bankruptcy. Others, like the *Rocky Mountain News*, have closed their doors for good. Newspaper circulation is nose-diving, and local radio and TV news seems headed in the same direction.

Our traditional media have been battered by a "perfect storm."

The rise of the Internet and the end of local advertising monopolies collided with the economic downturn.

But that's not the full story. We must also recognize that many of the industry's most serious wounds are self-inflicted.

Just a few years ago, the average profit margin for newspapers was 20 percent—with some raking in twice as much or more. Did they use these astronomical profits to invest in the quality of their products or to innovate for the future?

No. They just bought up more newspapers and TV stations.

While our regulators in Washington rubber-stamped these mega-mergers, the media companies took on massive amounts of debt. And they are now drowning in it.

Journalism Is a Public Service

But here's the dirty secret of the business: *Newspapers are still profitable.*

AdAge [*Advertising Age* magazine] recently reported that [media giant] McClatchy's papers earned a 21% profit margin last year [2008]; Gannet earned 18%—and yet they both still cut thousands and thousands of jobs.

Look—I'm not saying the business model isn't in trouble or that the ads are ever coming back. I'm certainly not saying the economy isn't in bad shape.

But if Washington hadn't looked the other way as these deals went through, newsrooms might have 10 years to experiment, adjust and adapt—instead of what feels like 10 minutes.

The last thing we need now is more of the same bad medicine that got us so sick in the first place. But that's exactly what the industry is asking for: weaker antitrust laws, cross-ownership, more and more consolidation

Doubling down on the bad policies of the past is exactly the wrong thing to do. As my colleague [and policy director at Free Press] Ben Scott told Congress a few weeks ago: Tying two rocks together won't help them float.

Some say do nothing. Let 'em drown. They point out that—from the run-up to the war in Iraq to the meltdown on Wall Street—the mainstream media haven't done their jobs.

Yet it's hard to imagine how we'd be better off with fewer journalists on the streets.

I believe journalism is indispensable in a democratic society. So if the market is failing, we may need to look elsewhere.

So what should we do?

First, we need to agree on what we're trying to save. This is not about newspapers—or not just about newspapers—it is about newsrooms and newsgathering.

This is not about protecting old institutions or propping up old business models. But it is about serving local communities.

It is about understanding that journalism is a public service—not just another business.

A National Strategy with Core Principles

The crisis in journalism is a national issue, and it requires a national solution. Just like we need a national plan to connect every American to affordable, high-speed Internet, we need a national strategy to make sure everyone can get quality news and information.

This national journalism strategy should be guided by core principles:

We must . . .

1. Protect the First Amendment. Free speech is essential to a free society and a functioning democracy. We need policies that protect and promote free speech.

We must . . .

2. Produce Quality Coverage. The public needs in-depth news on important local, national and international issues. They need diverse voices and viewpoints.

We must . . .

3. Provide Adversarial Perspectives. We need to hold the powerful accountable by scrutinizing government and corporations.

We must . . .

4. Promote Public Accountability. We need to treat journalism as a public service, not just another commodity.

We must . . .

5. Prioritize Innovation. We need to utilize new tools and technology to get journalism to the broadest range of people.

Unfortunately, up to this point, much of the debate over the future of journalism has fallen into two camps.

One believes the Internet is killing almost everything good about journalism.

But even if we could put the Internet back in the bottle, why would we ever want to?

The other camp believes the Internet will automatically and magically replace our current model of journalism with something better.

But the Internet alone won't meet our needs, for reasons starting with the fact that more than 40% of the country doesn't have access to broadband at home. As our news organizations collapse, it is cold comfort that someday sometime someone somewhere might replace them.

There is a fertile middle ground here—in which we can embrace digital technology and the promise of the Internet, while also sustaining vital professional journalism.

The key question is what are the models that can provide the institutional and financial support needed to keep skilled reporters on the beat? Or better yet, how can we put even more reporters on even more beats?

It's important to remember here that news has always been subsidized. But just because advertising no longer subsidizes journalism, does not mean that we no longer require news.

So we need to find new policies to support the media. And, yes, the government will probably have to be involved.

Of course, the government has always been involved in media policy. Back in the early days of the Republic, the question was whether we should mail all newspapers for free or just heavily subsidize them. Only the technology has changed.

There's no magic bullet here. No one-size-fits-all solution. We're going to have to experiment.

But here's what we know won't work: more media consolidation, of course, is not the answer.

This is not the time for a direct government bailout for [media mogul] Sam Zell or the *New York Times*.

Foundation money by itself won't do it. We don't endorse paywalls or mandatory micropayments that would cut off content from most of its audience.

Hiding from Google or suing bloggers for quoting you does not count as innovation.

Five Policies That Show Promise

But we've identified five policies—short-term and long-term—that we believe show the most promise.

In the short term:

1. New Ownership Models

—501(c)(3)s

—L3Cs

We need to take away some of the pressures from Wall Street and reinvest in serious journalism and in-depth reporting.

Nonprofit and low-profit models for news organizations could help balance between public needs and shareholder returns, giving them protections and advantages not available to the commercial press.

The nonprofit newspaper bill introduced by Senator [Ben] Cardin is a start—but it's too limited. Its language would largely exclude community newspapers and ethnic media. And it doesn't offer the same benefits to new media outlets and online news organizations as it would to the old broadsheets.

A possible alternative is the low-profit, limited liability corporation, or L3C—a structure now available in a few states that gives advantages to corporations committed to a social good and allows them to accept philanthropic support.

Newspapers operating as L3Cs could still earn a return for investors—but their social purpose would always trump the financial one.

2. New Incentives

—Divestiture

—Prepackaged bankruptcies

—Minority media tax certificate

As the biggest media companies collapse under their own weight, they will be forced to sell off properties. Usually this means selling to another big conglomerate or a private equity firm with no ties to the community.

Instead, we need a menu of options that would encourage media companies to sell off these properties to new owners who pledge to operate them in the public interest under a new structure like an L3C.

To do that we should refine existing bankruptcy and tax laws to encourage local investors, community groups or employees to take over failing news operations on favorable terms, keep journalists on the beat, and invest in local newsgathering.

Bankruptcy could be an opportunity in disguise. So-called prepackaged bankruptcies allow companies to negotiate and vote on reorganization plans before declaring bankruptcy. They are ideal for still viable businesses drowning in debt—like newspapers.

If done right, a failing paper could be bought up by a cooperative of its employees through a prepackaged bankruptcy, turned into a low-profit or tax-exempt organization; take money from philanthropists; and test ways to generate online revenue—all while still reporting and writing.

Likewise, we need to bring back proven policies like the minority media tax certificate to encourage the sale of media properties to under-represented groups.

Before it was eliminated in 1995, this policy—which gave tax benefits to those who sold media properties to racial and ethnic minorities—increased the number of broadcast licenses held by people of color by more than 700%.

3. Journalism Jobs Program

Our third proposal is to establish a journalism jobs program to train or retrain young or veteran journalists. We just passed a nearly trillion-dollar recovery package, but where are the reporters who should be watching how this money is being spent?

What if we took a few thousand AmeriCorps jobs and gave them to newsgathering organizations? And why not retrain veteran journalists with new media skills—to match their deep rolodexes of sources?

Or let's put them to work training our college students in media literacy. There's already a pilot program like that running at Stonybrook University.

Alternatively, the Department of Labor could design a program to help keep reporters employed—offsetting costs that would otherwise go to unemployment payments while keeping watchdogs on the beat.

These are short-term fixes. Over the longer term, we need to look at . . .

4. Journalism R&D [research and development] Fund

Just as government invests in medical research to heal the body, we need to invest in the experiments and new models that will heal the body politic.

We're calling for the development of a government-seeded innovation fund for journalism—a taxpayer-supported venture capital firm that invests in new journalism models. We propose starting this effort with a $50 million budget.

This fund—which could match private and public investment—would focus on new technology and startup initiatives, especially community-based newsrooms and outlets serving communities of color.

5. New Public Media

Finally . . .

Now is the time to re-imagine our current public broadcasting system and rebuild it as new public media with an overarching commitment to newsgathering and community service. . . .

Consider the numbers: We now spend just a little more than $400 million per year in public money for public media. That works out to just $1.35 per capita.

By comparison, Canada spends more than $22 per capita, and England spends $80 per capita.

With increased funding—say, to as little as $5 a person—the American public media system could dramatically increase its reach and relevance.

This money isn't just for journalism. Public media support arts, education and community service, too. Wouldn't you pay $5 for better media?

Think of it this way: Each of us spent $600 to bail out AIG [American International Group, a financial firm]. Five bucks for public media is a bargain.

Better yet, Congress should end the dance of annual appropriations and create a permanent trust fund that would remove public media from the political whims of Washington forever.

But it's not just about money. We also need to reform the governance structure of public media . . . we need to utilize new technology . . . we need to diversify the audience and programming . . . and we need to expand our definition of what public media is . . . not just PBS [Public Broadcasting Service] and NPR [National Public Radio], but Low Power FM [LPFM] stations, public access cable channels and independent Web sites.

One thing we can do right now is finally pass the bipartisan Local Community Radio Act and create hundreds of new LPFM stations.

It's been more than 40 years since the historic Carnegie Commission envisioned the public broadcasting system. We need President [Barack] Obama to establish a new White House commission to finally bring public media into the 21st century.

Leadership from the top is only part of the answer. To save the news and build the world-class public media system, we need broad public participation that's been missing from these crucial media debates for too long.

Journalists—many of whom were taught not to vote—are going to have to get involved in politics and policy if they want to keep their jobs. Public broadcasters are going to have reconnect with local communities.

Bloggers and grassroots media activists, academics and everyday people who believe the news should be more than traffic and weather and sports and who got kicked off *American Idol* last night are going to have to come together to build the political will for real change.

| "It is . . . far from clear that publicly funded news is superior to commercial news in serving the needs of a self-governing society."

Journalism Should Not Be Supported as a Public Service

Trevor Butterworth

In the following viewpoint, Trevor Butterworth opposes supporting journalism as a public service to preserve its future in the digital era. He contends that due to the lack of strategic and innovative ideas, news organizations are failing and do not deserve to be bailed out. Butterworth concludes that the real danger of public funding is how the public itself would have far-reaching demands that journalism be fair and free of bias. Trevor Butterworth is the editor of the website STAT, which investigates the use of statistics in the media and public policy.

As you read, consider the following questions:

1. How does Butterworth counter the argument that increasing content that is adversarial to the government is beneficial?

2. Why is persuading the public that journalism should be publicly funded a challenge, according to the author?

3. What evidence does Butterworth provide to bolster his assertion that the public would have far-reaching demands for fairness and accuracy if journalism were publicly funded?

For years, media leaders, editors and not a few reporters tried to ignore the coming digital storm, fiddling while technology transformed their world. Now, as that world evolves, the question is whether something greater is at risk from the new digital landscape: the future of journalism itself. What if the public won't buy into paywalled news? What if there really is no digital economy for the kind of reporting generally thought vital to the functioning of a democracy?

In a recent speech to the Federal Trade Commission, reprinted in the *Columbia Journalism Review*, Robert McChesney, a communications theorist, argued that this scenario should be seen as an eventuality rather than a probability; and that the consequences for democracy should force us all to reconceptualize journalism as "a public good, not a private good. It is," he continued, "like military defense, physical infrastructure, education, public health, and basic research. . . . it is something society requires, and people want, but the market cannot generate in sufficient quantity or quality. It requires government leadership to exist."

Technology Did Not Ruin Journalism

There are two obvious objections to this argument. The first is that journalism managed not only to adapt to the new-fangled technologies of photography, radio and television, but to be adapted by them. Eyewitness reporting developed through a symbiotic relationship with the telegraph, and not because it just seemed clever to show up to record events as they were happening. Mathew Brady didn't photograph the Civil War because the government thought it a good idea and issued a directive, but because he had made his fortune from photography and thought recording the war was a vital thing to do (it cost him his fortune and then the government short-changed him for the negatives in the resulting fire sale). Technology even changed the form of stories and the style of writing, because words were expensive to transmit and the telegraph was unreliable: Enter the inverted pyramid; exit adverbs and adjectives.

But technology didn't suddenly decide to ruin journalism—a generation of complacent news leaders simply failed to meet its challenges with the deft strategic thinking demanded by their pay scale. Why short their tech-savvy replacements by giving this old guard a bailout? Why default on the possibility that a better kind of "lookout on the ship of state" may emerge from the current maelstrom of innovation?

Publicly Funded News Is Not Superior

It is also far from clear that publicly funded news is superior to commercial news in serving the needs of a self-governing society. McChesney argues that as news subsidies have increased in Europe, "the content of news has become more adversarial toward the party in power and the government in general." But it's not certain that such adversarialism is always a boon for democracy. Publicly funded news organizations may want to prove their independence by being highly critical of government, but thinly veiled antagonism based on poor reporting or political prejudice has, for example, seriously damaged the BBC's [British Broadcasting Corporation] credibility.

At the same time, it's patently obvious that commercial news operations in Britain such as ITN [Independent Television News] and Sky are every bit as capable at broadcast journalism as their vast, publicly funded rival, and that this is simply a byproduct of competition. But commercial news is now at a distinct competitive disadvantage when you have a behemoth like the BBC "giving away" news on the Internet thanks to involuntary taxes that criminalize watching a television without a license. According to one poll, 50% of Britons want the license fee abolished.

Even if a voucher system were to replace direct government subsidy—as McChesney and his colleague John Nichols advocate in their book *The Death and Life of American Journalism*—and people were "free" to direct their $200 voucher to the media of their choice, where does this $40 billion come from? It's hard to escape the irony that at some point in the public accounts you have, in red ink, a coercively funded free press—if enough people, that is, bother to redeem their vouchers (something that shouldn't be banked on).

Any one of these reasons may be sufficient to oppose the government stepping in to fund journalism (it could also be argued that government should spend the money instead on making itself more open); but there is a deeper conceptual problem lurking in the idea that journalism should be turned into a public good, like health or defense.

Public vs. Private

As the philosopher Raymond Geuss notes in [his book] *Public Goods, Private Goods*, the definitions of "public" and "private" are not fixed in separate realms, with defined borders: "It is not," he writes, "that we discover what the distinction is between the public and private and then proceed to determine what value attitudes we should have to it, but rather that given our values and knowledge we decide what sorts of things we think need regulating or caring for—and then stamp them 'public.'"

For example, your finances are not "public" in the sense that anyone ought to be able to see them; but that notion of privacy doesn't extend to a politician taking a kickback. Similarly, your voting preferences and even political values are essentially private. But does that notion of privacy extend to the political beliefs and values of journalists? Many journalists would say, yes, there is a professional firewall between private belief and the practice of journalism. Many non-journalists would say, no; this is what accounts for so much bias in reporting—and the conflict of interest between the private belief and reporting should be made explicit.

How does public funding alter this clash between the private and the public in journalism?

Given that the press is held in abysmally low regard by the American public, as delineated in survey upon survey, it would be hard to divert taxpayer money without demanding some public accountability. Why? Because all such public goods—national security, public education, health and infrastructure—are held accountable through some kind of regulation; that is the price of government funding—and why should journalism paid for by the people be any different? Oh, yes, cite the First Amendment: But it is hard to see how you could persuade people that public funding for journalism is a good idea without more robust protection from invasions of privacy, abuses from dilatory or inaccurate reporting, and political bias.

The Real Danger of Public Funding

The dangers of public funding are usually framed in terms of government interference and looming authoritarianism; but the real danger is that the public will demand procedural justice that will go far beyond the sop of an ombudsman. In fact, in 1997, and at a time when public opinion was much more favorable toward the press than it is now [in 2010], a Harris Poll conducted for the Center for Media and Public Affairs found that 84% of the public favored a government "fairness doctrine" requiring equal treatment of all sides in controversies, while 70% believed that courts should impose fines for "biased or inaccurate" journalism. As one wit said, "it would be easier to regard journalism as a public good if the public thought it was any good."

But has journalism reached such a point of utter failure that we are ready to take these risks and hit the panic button? Maybe, if you are sitting at one of the publications where your boss is stuck in 1993, it could feel that way. But the government isn't like Batman, who returns to being Bruce Wayne once the crisis of the moment is over; ask for government help and government will keep helping until it hurts. McChesney's arguments are those of a generation exiting the media. Perhaps, it might be better for the future of journalism if they all hurried up.

Periodical and Internet Sources Bibliography

The following articles have been selected to supplement the diverse views presented in this chapter.

Kate Bulkley "The Rise of Citizen Journalism," *The Guardian* (Manchester, UK), June 10, 2012.

Ted Diadiun "Rise of 'Citizen Journalists' Hasn't Eliminated the Need for Professional Journalists: Ted Diadiun," Cleveland.com, September 14, 2013.

The Digital Journal "Let's Abolish the Term 'Citizen Journalist,'" December 2009. http://digitaljournal.com.

Susan Enfield "My Defense of Scholastic Journalism," *School Administrator*, March 2013.

Julia Haskins "Opinion: In Defense of Journalism School," USA Today College, August 10, 2012. www.usatodayeducate.com.

Trevor Knoblich "Can Citizen Journalism Move Beyond Crisis Reporting?" *Idea Lab* (blog), Public Broadcasting Service, May 9, 2013. www.pbs.org.

Ombline Lucas "Citizen Journalists: A New Kind of War Reporting," *Red Cross Red Crescent*, no. 2, 2012.

Peter McAllister "Degree of Doubt for Journalism Students," *The Australian*, April 12, 2012.

Hanna Nikkanen "They Shoot Citizen Journalists, Don't They? Curating or Outsourcing? Opportunities and Threats in Post-gatekeeper Journalism," International Federation of Library Associations and Institutions, December 10, 2012. www.ifla.org.

Jenn Prentice "Degrees Are Useless, and Other Tips for Aspiring Journalists," Business Insider, June 16, 2011. www.businessinsider.com.

OPPOSING
VIEWPOINTS®
SERIES

CHAPTER 3

How Should Journalists Be Protected?

Chapter Preface

In November 2011, Crystal Cox, a self-proclaimed investigative blogger, was found guilty of libel by an Oregon federal court. She was fined $2.5 million for defaming Kevin Padrick, an attorney for the Obsidian Finance Group. On one of her websites, obsidianfinancesucks.com, Cox branded Padrick a "thug" and a "thief," alleging that he had committed tax fraud. When Padrick sued for defamation, Cox sought journalist's protection under Oregon's shield law to not identify her sources. In his ruling against Cox, federal judge Marco A. Hernandez described the qualifications of a journalist, including an education in journalism, credentials or evidence of an association with a known news agency, and evidence that "the other side" was contacted so both sides of the story or issue could be presented. "If only I had a journalist degree . . . i can bE as sMart as all you real JournaLists," Cox later wrote in her blog. She also wrote, "And maybe if I had them there 'standards of journalism' I could learn how to call Both sides and get some statement they claim to be true and then well put my twist on it and put it into the Traditional Media machine and wala it comes out as Accredited, Protected, Real Legitimate News."[1]

Some commentators disagree with Hernandez's definition of a journalist, asserting that, if widely applied, it would have negative impacts on reporting in the digital age. "The court's unnecessary and rigid definition of 'media' may harm others who in the future want to communicate important information to the public through the Internet while protecting the identity of their sources," argue Trevor Timm and Matt Zimmerman of the Electronic Frontier Foundation, a digital rights

---

1. Crystal Cox, "So If I Am Not Media, and Don't Have the Power That Media Does Then How Did What I Write Affect Obsidian Finance in Any Way?," *Obsidian Finance Sucks* (blog), December 8, 2011. www.obsidianfinancesucks.blogspot.com.

group. They continue, "Journalism is not limited to a particular medium; instead, it focuses on whether someone is engaged in gathering information and disseminating it to the public."[2]

However, when Hernandez denied Cox's motion for a new trial, he agreed that bloggers can be considered journalists. In his ruling he writes, "In my discussion, I did not state that a person who 'blogs' could never be considered 'media.' I also did not state that to be considered 'media,' one had to possess all or most of the characteristics I recited." He points out that the evidence against Cox demonstrated that she was not a journalist: After posting her damaging blog, she had approached the Obsidian Finance Group with an offer to repair the damage for a fee. Hernandez writes, "Rather, I confined my conclusion to the record defendant created in this case and noted that defendant had presented no evidence as to any single one of the characteristics which would tend to establish oneself as a member of the 'media.'"[3] The authors in this chapter debate how and whether journalists should be protected for doing their jobs.

2. Trevor Timm and Matt Zimmerman, "The Crystal Cox Case and Bloggers as Journalists," Electronic Frontier Foundation, December 13, 2011. www.eff.org/deeplinks/2011/12/crystal-cox-and-bloggers-as-journalists.
3. *Obsidian Finance Group, LLC, and Kevin D. Padrick v. Crystal Cox*, March 27, 2012. http://ia700403.us.archive.org.

> *"Enacting a robust federal shield law for reporters has obvious merits and no partisan impediments. It is thus necessary and doable."*

Reporters Need a Federal Shield Law

David B. Rivkin Jr. and Lee A. Casey

In the following viewpoint, David B. Rivkin Jr. and Lee A. Casey argue that a federal shield law, or reporter's privilege, to protect the confidentiality of news sources is vital to journalism. They explain that shield laws are currently different in each state and applied in courts on an individual basis. Rivkin and Casey conclude that a federal shield law is necessary because journalism serves a national market and that such a law would be consistent with how laws on other issues balance justice with constitutional and societal values. David B. Rivkin Jr. and Lee A. Casey are attorneys and partners in the BakerHostetler law firm in Washington, DC.

As you read, consider the following questions:

1. Why would a federal shield law not violate the constitutional protections against federalism, according to Rivkin and Casey?

2. How to do the authors address the concern that reporter's privilege will impede the government and plaintiffs in the courts?

3. According to Rivkin and Casey, in what cases should a federal shield law not be extended?

A Colorado judge's threatened contempt sanctions against Fox News investigative reporter Jana Winter—who refuses to reveal a confidential news source—has refocused public attention on how journalists operate.

News must often be gathered from confidential sources, or not at all. Given how vital is the freedom of the press in a democracy, that confidentiality must be maintained. It is time that Congress recognize this and enact legislation that enables journalists to protect their confidential sources and newsgathering materials.

Ms. Winter covered the July 20, 2012, mass shooting that killed 12 people and injured 58 others in an Aurora, Colo., movie theater. Based on confidential law-enforcement sources, she reported that James E. Holmes, who is charged with the murders, had previously sent a notebook to his psychiatrist describing his intent to kill.

Now that Mr. Holmes is facing trial, his defense attorneys want to know the identities of Ms. Winter's sources to aid in their client's defense. The judge has yet to decide whether the notebook, which is potentially covered by a patient-psychiatrist privilege, is admissible. He has postponed until August a decision on whether he will force Ms. Winter to reveal her sources. But if he ultimately sides with the defendant, Ms. Winter will have to choose between violating her sources' trust and going to jail.

Such pressures on reporters are not uncommon, with prosecutors, defense counsel and judges demanding disclosure of their confidential sources and newsgathering materials. In 2005, for instance, *New York Times* reporter Judith Miller was

© Baylor University/Claire Taylor, Lariat Staff.

jailed for refusing to reveal a confidential source, who leaked to her the identity of CIA employee Valerie Plame, to a grand jury.

Congress Should Do More

Although most states provide some protection for journalists in the form of a reporter's "privilege," or "shield law," the extent of these provisions varies. Fewer than half of the states (including such key media markets as New York, California and Washington, D.C.) have a robust privilege that protects journalists' confidential sources, with a few narrow exceptions. Other states have recognized only a "qualified" privilege, where consideration is given to how difficult it might be to otherwise obtain the desired information.

David S. Tatel, a highly respected judge of the U.S. Court of Appeals for the D.C. Circuit, suggested in Ms. Miller's case—where contempt sanctions were upheld because of the gravity of the national security issues involved—that "reason and experience," as manifested by the laws in "forty-nine states and the District of Columbia," support "recognition of a privilege for reporters' confidential source." Unfortunately, today federal law recognizes only a modest reporter's privilege, grounded in the rules of evidence and applied by courts on a case-by-case basis, without detailed congressional guidance. Congress can and should do more, defining such a privilege by statute.

A national privilege should include a presumption that journalists may protect the confidentiality of their sources and that this privilege can be overridden only when there would otherwise be an imminent danger to public safety or national security (such as the actual threat of violence or attack). Confidentiality would not be overridden merely because it might jeopardize a prosecution or civil lawsuit.

A national law would not violate the Constitution's fundamental federalism principles. States are guaranteed wide latitude in addressing their own needs and concerns. But where a national market has developed—as is the case with news and newsgathering—a uniform federal approach to regulation is justifiable.

Federal pre-emption of state law in this area will be a step further than Congress has considered in the past, but Congress has wrestled with this problem before. A bill that would have applied to all federal proceedings, establishing a robust privilege subject to a few exceptions, came close to passage in 2009. It foundered because of the "WikiLeaks" controversy, where a trove of the most sensitive U.S. diplomatic and military documents was released en masse. The bill's defeat may well have been Julian Assange's ultimate revenge against the freedom of the press that he disingenuously claimed to venerate.

A reporter's privilege is not cost-free—sometimes it will impede the ability of the government and private plaintiffs to win in court. However, the cause of justice is not the only worthwhile goal in America's system of ordered liberty. Civil and criminal prosecutions are already hampered by a set of well-recognized privileges—accorded to psychiatrists, priests, lawyers and spouses—that reflect a societal recognition that they are worth the costs.

Similarly, prosecutors are often unable to introduce important evidence if it was improperly obtained, reflecting the belief that inculcating proper behavior by law-enforcement personnel is worth the costs. A strong federal shield law for reporters would be consistent with how we balance the cause of justice and other key constitutional and societal values.

Given the growing importance of nontraditional media sources, the privilege should apply to professional reporters and citizen-bloggers. It should not, however, be extended to cases where the reporter himself is the target of a criminal investigation unrelated to his receiving of confidential information, such as securities trading on inside information.

Enacting a robust federal shield law for reporters has obvious merits and no partisan impediments. It is thus necessary and doable.

| *"[A] wise federal shield law is difficult to draft."*

A Federal Shield Law, Potentially a Slippery Slope

Walter Pincus

In the following viewpoint, Walter Pincus asserts that enacting a federal shield law, or reporter's privilege, to protect confidential sources would be a slippery slope toward the government's targeting of journalists with certain organizational associations. Congress's previous efforts to enact a shield law have included dangerous standards for defining which journalists are protected. Non-covered journalists may include reporters from foreign press agencies or with ties to civil rights groups or marginalized political organizations. Walter Pincus is a columnist for the Washington Post *who covers issues of intelligence, defense, and foreign policy.*

As you read, consider the following questions:

1. How does Pincus counter the argument that a federal shield law is needed to prevent reporters from being automatically subpoenaed in state courts?

2. What objection does the author have to a federal shield law concerning media lobbyists?

3. What is Pincus's opinion of national security reporters who protect their sources?

The siren song of a congressionally drafted federal shield law has arrived to answer the news media's cries for help.

I turn to the adage, "Be careful what you wish for."

First, let's deal with the standard argument that if the District of Columbia and 49 states (all except Wyoming) can have shield laws, why not the federal government?

One answer is that since most criminal and civil cases go through state courts, shield laws at that level are needed to prevent prosecutors or lawyers from automatically subpoenaing reporters who have covered events, talked to witnesses, gathered records and done work that those involved in such cases otherwise would have to do.

But states do not generate the same sort of national security and confidential-source criminal issues as those at the center of the contests between the media and the Justice Department. The Supreme Court made it clear in the 1972 Branzburg decision that the First Amendment is no protection for a journalist called to testify before a federal grand jury in a criminal case.

In recent decisions, some lower-court federal judges have indicated a path to some sort of common law privilege for journalists, but a federal shield law has over time seemed like a quicker route.

The late, great journalist Anthony Lewis, who wrote the book about the First Amendment, rightly said in 2007 during a panel titled "Are Journalists Privileged?" that "a wise federal shield law is difficult to draft." During that panel at the Benjamin Cardoza School of Law, he cited as one "inescapable problem": "defining who is a journalist."

Lewis—and others—focused mainly on those hundreds of thousands of individuals who publish news, commentary and photographs on the Internet.

I have a different worry: that Congress in past federal shield law efforts has tried to regulate who the protected journalists will be by using more dangerous standards. The slippery slope of standards has involved such things as who the journalists work for or their organizational associations.

The White House last week asked Sen. Charles E. Schumer (D-N.Y.) to take the lead in developing a shield law similar to one he sponsored that passed the Senate Judiciary Committee in 2009. On the CBS program *Face the Nation* on Sunday, Schumer said he would work with a new bipartisan "Gang of Eight" on a bill that would require the government in each case to go to a judge who would balance the need to find a leaker against the journalist's desire to protect sources.

But Schumer's earlier effort excluded from being a journalist, or "covered person," individuals on or "reasonably likely to be" on various government lists.

For example, it eliminated a person who is an "agent of a foreign power," as defined by the Foreign Intelligence Surveillance Act of 1978. That definition would include a person working for "an entity that is openly acknowledged by a foreign government or governments to be directed and controlled by such foreign government or governments."

The legislators apparently were after Al Jazeera, partially owned by the government of Qatar, and perhaps the Iranian government-owned news services. But wouldn't that also mean journalists from the BBC, Agence France-Presse and some Russian government-owned services?

Other non-covered journalists were those "reasonably likely" to be working for groups on the State Department's list of foreign terrorist organizations or Treasury's Specially Designated Global Terrorist list, and anyone "attempting the crime of providing material support" to a terrorist group or anyone

The Responsibility in Using Confidential Sources

Beyond the question of whether shield laws actually work, it's well worth discussing whether journalists have a responsibility to use confidential sources much less often than they have done and to make sure that if they do, it is (1) as a last resort rather than as a lazy way to avoid hard-nosed reporting efforts; and (2) in regard to topics that are seriously important to the public. I believe strongly that journalists must improve in these areas—as a matter of ethics; to protect their credibility with the public and to avoid creating situations where courts can too easily rule against them and against their colleagues who may need to rely on confidential sources in the future.

A. David Gordon, Controversies in Media Ethics, *2011.*

"aiding, abetting, or conspiring in illegal activity with a person or organization" on any terrorist list.

As I wrote about the first Schumer bill, what if it had been proposed in the 1950s, when Congress would have excluded from its journalist designation anyone associated with the Communist Party or liberal groups designated as fellow travelers? In the 1960s and 1970s, it probably would have excluded those associated with anti-Vietnam War groups or radical civil rights organizations.

Who would be added to such a list by a future Congress?

As others have noted, Schumer's bill would not have prevented Justice from getting the Associated Press phone records or the e-mails of Fox News' James Rosen. Perhaps it could have delayed things for months or years, but who would have benefited from that?

Another of my old objections to a federal shield law is that it results in media lobbyists going to Congress to seek a privilege from the lawmakers journalists cover. The attorney-client privilege in federal law and those granted clergy, doctors and social workers all arose out of judicial decisions, not from lawmakers.

And why are we seeking a federal shield law now? The leaker or leakers in the AP and Fox stories were not whistle-blowers exposing government malfeasance. They passed classified materials in violation of criminal law. These journalists were witnesses to those violations and should be treated like other citizens.

National security reporters protect their sources and should take the same chances with the law as those who provide them with classified information. Max Frankel, former executive editor of the *New York Times* who appeared with Lewis at that 2007 Cardoza panel, put it this way: "The law is especially political and there is no law that we could write to address this issue, especially when you wave national security in front of the judges."

He added that no judge could do the balancing between harm to the national security and informing the public, since "no one can anticipate the ultimate consequence of any given story."

Frankel said, "At certain moments, if the country is panicked with fear, it may be willing to put a reporter or two in jail. So be it. The contest must go on. It is a political contest for which . . . the law has no answer."

I'll go along with Frankel: As he put it, "I trust the politics of this game to decide the issue in each generation of journalists."

| "The United States requires a Supreme
Court willing to deepen protections for
investigative reporters."

Journalists Should Have Greater Legal Protection

Steve Coll

In the following viewpoint, Steve Coll states that the free speech rights of journalists have been increasingly restricted under President Barack Obama's administration. He asserts that the federal government has recently undertaken the most aggressive media subpoena in decades, placed a reporter under surveillance, and prosecuted a record number of governmental officials for providing information to the media. Coll concludes that the US Supreme Court needs to increase protections for journalists. Steve Coll is president and chief executive officer of the think tank the New American Foundation and a staff writer for the New Yorker *magazine.*

As you read, consider the following questions:

1. According to Coll, what is significant about the opinion in *Branzburg v. Hayes?*

2. How does the author defend the Associated Press's story on an Al Qaeda bomb plot, which resulted in a subpoena of telephone records?

3. What is Coll's view of a federal shield law?

In 1969, when nothing excited the public's interest like the depredations of drug fiends, the Louisville *Courier-Journal* sent a reporter named Paul Branzburg to penetrate Kentucky's marijuana underground. He published eyewitness accounts; a photograph accompanying one of them showed hands hovering over a pile of hashish. A grand jury ordered him to identify the dealers he had met. He refused. *Branzburg v. Hayes* landed at the Supreme Court three years later. Justice Byron White wrote, in a 5–4 opinion, that the First Amendment does not exempt reporters from giving evidence in criminal cases. Yet the Court also held that the Constitution protects reporters from indiscriminate government subpoenas. The opinion is regarded today as a muddle; it does not make clear how much protection journalists deserve. The Supreme Court has yet to revisit the issue.

In reaction to *Branzburg*, the Justice Department enacted new guidelines for federal prosecutors seeking evidence from journalists. They are far from ideal—they have loopholes that give an Attorney General wide discretion. Yet they have often discouraged Justice from overreaching. The guidelines require that the Attorney General sign off on all media subpoenas, that any demands "be as narrowly drawn as possible," and that, in all but the most exceptional cases, news organizations be notified of a subpoena, giving them time to appeal it in court.

Aggressive Seizure and Surveillance

Last month [May 2013], President [Barack] Obama's Attorney General, Eric Holder, admitted that earlier this year Justice had secretly subpoenaed two months of records for twenty telephone lines used by Associated Press [A.P.] reporters and editors. It was the most aggressive known federal seizure of media records since the [President Richard M.] Nixon Administration. Holder has said that he recused himself from the case, though the circumstances remain unclear. But Justice offered the A.P. no chance to appeal the action, and only by authoritarian twists of logic could a secret subpoena seeking such diverse records be construed as the narrowest course possible. In a letter to Holder, the Reporters Committee for Freedom of the Press wrote that the action "calls into question the very integrity of Department of Justice policies toward the press."

The subpoena arose from a 2012 story about how the C.I.A.'s infiltration of an Al Qaeda affiliate in Yemen had thwarted a bombing plot. The A.P.'s scoop may have angered the C.I.A. because such disclosures can endanger sources, but the A.P. held the story for five days to allow the [Obama] Administration to prepare. And, after the story's publication, John Brennan, at that time Obama's counterterrorism chief and now the director of the C.I.A., touted the success of the operation that the A.P. described, without citing any damage to national security.

Also last month, the press revealed that F.B.I. agents had reviewed the comings and goings of the Fox News reporter James Rosen when he visited the State Department to conduct interviews with a source helping him with a story on North Korea's nuclear program. Holder approved an affidavit for a search warrant that named Rosen as a possible co-conspirator in violation of the Espionage Act, because he might have received classified information while doing his job.

Departing from First Amendment Norms

It has been apparent for several years that the Obama Administration has departed from the First Amendment norms established during the seven Presidencies since *Branzburg*.

Holder has overseen six prosecutions of government officials for aiding the press, more than were brought by all previous Administrations combined. Even after the A.P. controversy erupted, Obama said that he would make "no apologies" for zealous press-leak investigations, since unauthorized disclosures of secrets jeopardized the lives of the soldiers and the spies he sent in danger's way.

It seems likely that Holder or his deputies have authorized other press subpoenas and surveillance regimes that have not yet been disclosed. The Justice Department has acted belligerently even in cases where no grave harm to the public interest has been demonstrated, or where, as in the A.P. case, the leaks under suspicion have served to publicize the Administration's successes. Why would the President preside over such illiberal decisions? His longest-serving advisers are disciplined and insular to a fault; press leaks offend their aesthetic of power. And it would hardly be surprising if Obama viscerally disdained the media's self-important excesses. Yet the Administration's record cannot be chalked up to the President's temperament or to Holder's poor judgment alone.

It is no coincidence that the A.P. and the Fox cases arose from national-security reporting. Obama inherited a bloated national-security state. It contains far too many official secrets and far too many secret-keepers—more than a million people now hold top-secret clearances. Under a thirty-year-old executive order issued by the White House, the intelligence agencies must inform the Justice Department whenever they believe that classified information has been disclosed illegally to the press. These referrals operate on a kind of automatic pilot, and the system is unbalanced. Prosecutors in Justice's national-security division initially decide on whether to make a criminal case or to defer to the First Amendment. The record shows that in recent years the division has been bent on action.

Last month, at the National Defense University, Obama pledged to end America's formal war on terrorist groups. His speech was one of the most impressive of his second term. He announced renewed plans to close Guantánamo [the US military prison located on Guantánamo Bay Naval Base in Cuba], and he promised to tighten the rules governing classified drone strikes. He made no mention, though, of the many examples of investigative reporting—about the torture and abuse of prisoners, about official lies issued by the [George W.] Bush Administration on the road to war in Iraq, about targeting errors in drone attacks—that have helped to discredit the policies he now seeks to wind down.

An Unfettered Press Is Vital

In the long run, to rebalance the national-security state and to otherwise revitalize American democracy, the United States requires a Supreme Court willing to deepen protections for investigative reporters, as the majority in *Branzburg* would not. In response to criticism about the A.P. case, Obama has reintroduced federal legislation that would clarify journalists' rights. Such a federal "shield law" might be constructive, but new legislation with overly broad national-security exceptions would be even worse than the status quo.

The President remarked recently that an unfettered press is vital because it "helps hold me accountable, helps hold our government accountable, and helps our democracy function." The media are not just watchdogs barking at the White House and the C.I.A. The First Amendment aspires to a fuller compact among citizens, including between journalists and confidential sources, that is premised on the self-evident truth that secrecy and concentrated power are inherently corrupting.

| *"When the press demands or assumes special privileges, we are forced back to the question of who is the press."*

Who Owns the First Amendment?

Michael Kinsley

In the following viewpoint, written in 2010, Michael Kinsley maintains that journalists frequently exploit the First Amendment when investigating the government. He also criticizes the protection of anonymous sources through reporter's privilege, stating that journalists should not have the power to decide which sources should remain anonymous. Kinsley concludes that with the advent of the Internet, determining who is a journalist has become harder and that the courts may soon be overwhelmed with all kinds of people claiming to be journalists and seeking protection. Michael Kinsley is a political journalist and commentator.

As you read, consider the following questions:

1. How does FOIA affect journalists and government agencies, according to Kinsley?

2. According to the author, what do many journalists believe about reporter's privilege?

3. What bothers Kinsley the most about "the cult of the source"?

The Freedom of Information Act (FOIA, pronounced "*foy-ah*") is one of the most important weapons in the reporter's arsenal. Essentially, and with lots of exceptions and exclusions, it requires the government to supply documents on request. Journalism schools offer courses on how to file a FOIA request. Many exposés of official misbehavior would be impossible without FOIA. It's almost like a subpoena power for journalists. It's also a tremendous burden on government agencies—and some of its biggest users are not journalists but companies trolling for commercial information about their rivals.

California's state version of FOIA is called the Public Records Act. Last fall, for reasons too boring to go into, an aide to State Attorney General (and once and possibly future governor) Jerry Brown covertly taped and transcribed a conversation with a reporter. (Taping phone conversations without the consent of everyone on the call is supposed to be illegal in California.) Several California papers requested this transcript as well as those of any other covertly taped phone conversations between journalists and the state attorney general's office. The results included four interviews with Brown himself. Brown always "gives good quote," as they say, and the dean of the Sacramento press corps, George Skelton of the *Los Angeles Times*, got a nice juicy column out of the transcripts. Nevertheless, he admitted,

> it still makes me cringe. The public records act seems to be running amok when a reporter's private interview with a public figure can be handed over to competitors . . . I'm no lawyer, but it seems to me that a reporter's interview with a

government official is not public business. It's not like awarding contracts, appointing cronies or appeasing contributors.

Actually, it's very much like all those things. An interview is a commercial transaction in which the reporter and the source each hope to gain something. Such exchanges rarely amount to anything illicit, but most FOIA requests, on all subjects, are dry holes. And many FOIA requests offend people's sense of privacy or give succor to their enemies, rivals, or competitors. Now, Skelton knows how it feels, and he's honest enough to say that he doesn't like it (though in this case he benefited from it). But he never felt the law had "run amok" until it intruded (at least potentially) on his own commercial privacy. . . .

More to the point, even if you could successfully draw that line between journalists and everybody else, why should you? Journalists' special pleading is one reason we are so unpopular.

A final example concerns that hoary subject: anonymous sources. Like FOIA, anonymous sources are vital to journalists' task of monitoring the behavior of government and powerful private institutions. Many journalists believe passionately that a "journalist's privilege"—like the privileges for spouses, ministers, lawyers, and so on—should protect them from having to reveal the identity of their sources in criminal trials and other circumstances where nonjournalists must talk or risk punishment. Many journalists, in fact, believe that such a right is already part of the First Amendment, if only judges would recognize it. The Supreme Court has turned down opportunities to recognize such a right (which would be a right *not* to speak, in contrast with the First Amendment's usual concern with a right *to* speak), but most states have enacted "shield" laws allowing journalists to protect their sources to one degree or another.

You cannot deny the sincerity or seriousness of journalists on this issue. Many—most notably Judith Miller of *The New York Times*—have gone to jail rather than break a promise of anonymity to a source. But you also cannot deny the arrogance of the absolutism here. The question is not whether journalists should be forced to break promises to anonymous sources. The question is whether they should have made these promises in the first place, and whether sometimes they should be happy to break them. The whole saga (which also involved other journalists: Matthew Cooper of *Time*, the late Robert Novak, and so on) concerned the "outing" of a CIA agent, Valerie Plame. (It's all coming back now. Right?) The CIA also has its secrets—legitimate secrets. Do the legitimate secrets of *The New York Times* always trump the legitimate secrets of the CIA? And why do reporters continue to owe protection to sources who turn out to be lying, or to be part of an official disinformation campaign rather than brave dissidents?

And does the press always get to decide whose secrets trump? What bothers me most about the cult of the source is the press's insistence on its right to ignore due process of law and refuse to reveal sources even after the issue has been fully litigated. Fine: appeal it up to the Supreme Court if you want, but in a democracy with an (all but) uncorrupted judiciary, if you ultimately lose, you should obey the law as it is, not as you would like it to be. Especially if you are concurrently publishing editorials urging this course on the president of the United States (as *The Times* and other publications were doing about George W. Bush during Plamegate).

When the press demands or assumes special privileges, we are forced back to the question of who is the press, and to Justice Kennedy's puckish point that the Internet is making this distinction harder. The Senate Judiciary Committee has passed a national shield law that is not absolutist. It lists various circumstances in which the reporter's privilege will not be recognized, such as preventing "destruction of critical infrastructure." And it defines a journalist with elegant simplicity as a person who has the intent to disseminate information to the public. This definition is good, though you have to wonder who would *not* qualify for the privilege under its terms. Federal courts may soon be flooded with witnesses who are bloggers from mymafia.com. And then there is the question of why any journalist who is also a citizen and a human being would even want to keep secret the identity of someone who is planning to destroy critical infrastructure.

"*[For] a journalist on a dangerous professional assignment . . . knowing the law may spell the difference between getting killed and staying alive.*"

Journalists Covering Armed Conflicts Need to Know the Law

Red Batario

In the following viewpoint, written in 2007, Red Batario explains that journalists covering conflict areas around the world face great danger. He maintains that even though journalists are not combatants in the conflict, they may be kidnapped, injured, or killed just for being there. Batario concludes that journalists need to know and understand the laws, treaties, and conventions that can protect them as they work in conflict areas. Red Batario is the Southeast Asia regional coordinator for the International News Safety Institute, a nonprofit, nonpartisan organization that works to protect journalists around the world. He is also the executive director of the Center for Community Journalism and Development, a nonprofit media organization.

As you read, consider the following questions:

1. What effect do violent attacks on journalists have, according to Batario?

2. Why, according to the author, are local journalists and newsgathering teams covering armed conflicts at a disadvantage?

3. According to Batario, why are journalists working with troops on the frontlines not protected by law?

Journalists today face a broad range of conflict situations that are extremely complex and confusing. From conventional wars with defined battle lines to acts of terrorism that blur boundaries, from banditry to extremism or even pocket wars between feuding clans, journalists have to put themselves in ever increasing danger to get the story out.

Over the last 10 years [1996–2006] more than 1,000 journalists and media staff worldwide have been killed in the line of duty. In many parts of the globe, especially the Philippines, coping with threats, harassment, intimidation or worse has become part of the journalist's job description.

Journalists, especially those who cover conflict and other dangerous environments, can never be completely safe. It is their job to be in the danger zone to bring to the public's attention the progress of international and national conflicts. Their work often requires them to expose wrongdoing, to open for public scrutiny what some people would prefer to keep hidden. This puts them at grave risk. And the risks have become terribly high.

The International News Safety Institute (INSI) points out, "as modern warfare, terrorism and crime follow different patterns, journalists reporting these conflicts and events are ever more at risk of being caught in a crossfire or taken hostage. The free flow of information, on which enlightened governments and peoples depend, suffers." Violent attacks on journalists tend to have a chilling effect. Attacks hamper the journalists' ability to probe deeply and report accurately thus depriving the public of its right to know.

Article 19 of the [United Nations] Universal Declaration of Human Rights adopted on December 10, 1948, states that journalists have the right to "seek, receive, and impart information." This right is restated in the International Covenant on Civil and Political Rights which has been signed or ratified by more than 140 states, and in several regional conventions and charters, such as the European Convention for the Protection of Human Rights and the African Charter of Human and People's Rights.

To exercise this right journalists often have to put themselves in harm's way. But the exercise of this right should be viewed in the context of modern conflict situations that journalists may find themselves covering or reporting on.

Understanding Conflict

"In terms of international law, there are three broad categories of conflict which journalists may encounter. Superimposed on any of these broad categories there can be additional threats of violence posed, for example, by terrorism, extremist ideology, and insurgency."

International armed conflict—arises when one State uses armed force against another State or several others. Both sides are clearly defined and militaries wear different and distinct uniforms. There are identifiable front lines and the armed forces follow a chain of command. Parties to the conflict are generally aware of their obligations under international humanitarian law.

Internal armed conflict—occurs within the territory of the State and does not involve the military of another State. In many instances, the armed forces of the State are used against dissident forces, rebel or insurgent groups as in the case of the New People's Army (NPA) and the Moro Islamic Liberation

Front (MILF) in the Philippines, to cite some examples. In other cases, there are two or more armed groups fighting within the State but not necessarily involving the armed forces, like what is happening in East Timor.

If the opposition forces are better organized, have a clear command-and-control structure, and have the ability to carry out military operations and even, to some extent, operate a system of governance, slightly different provisions of the law apply. Each belligerent party is "bound to apply, as a minimum, the fundamental humanitarian provisions of international law contained in Article 3 common to all four Geneva Conventions."

Internal disturbances and tensions—a situation usually referred to by the military as "internal security operations" such as mass arrests, violent demonstrations and riots, proclaiming a state of emergency, large numbers of persons detained for long periods, ill-treatment and torture of detainees, harassment of journalists and lawyers representing detainees or suspects or drawing attention to repression, allegations of forced disappearances or unlawful killings.

Internal disturbances and tensions are not covered by international humanitarian law but by international human rights law and standards and the domestic laws of the State.

In the Line of Fire

By the very nature of their work journalists and media staff must be at the forefront of unfolding events, be it something mundane as a ribbon-cutting ceremony for a new government program or something life-threatening like the eruption of hostilities between two warring forces.

Journalists covering armed conflict and investigating human rights violations are of course open to greater dangers such as getting caught in a cross fire or being targeted. Those who embed with armed forces or cover the frontlines are particularly vulnerable to physical harm.

During a news safety conference and training last December [2006] in Bali for Southeast Asian frontline journalists organized by INSI, a female reporter from an Indonesian television station narrated how she was kidnapped and held for seven days in Iraq by insurgents.

She was after a story that would have helped people understand not only the horrors of war but also the often horrific acts committed by combatants in defiance of international humanitarian law.

In an extract from the International Review of the Red Cross in 1983, Alain Modoux, head of the ICRC [International Committee of the Red Cross] Information Department, wrote: "let us not forget that under Article 85 of Protocol I, the most serious of these violations are considered as war crimes. Whenever journalists witness such violations, it is therefore their duty to report them. I am convinced that public opinion, conditioned by the media, is an excellent means of bringing pressure to bear on belligerents and is capable of favorably modifying the attitude of combatants to victims protected by humanitarian law."

But this often comes with a huge price tag for journalists in armed conflict situations: injury or death.

As had been pointed out earlier, journalists covering armed conflict are constantly exposed to physical dangers and can become victims of the direct effects of hostilities like getting caught in a bombing raid or artillery barrage, being hit by shrapnel from a mortar round or by a stray bullet.

Journalists can also become victims of arbitrary arrest, physical abuse such as torture, disappearance, etc. by authorities, in particular the military, police or paramilitaries operating in the conflict area.

It is interesting to note that the International Federation of Journalists (IFJ) has pointed out that of the more than 1,192 journalists killed worldwide [from 1990 to 2002] more than 90 per cent were born and grew up in the land where

Unlike Civilians, Unlike Soldiers

By the very nature of their work, the categorization of journalists and media workers seems to fall between the two main actors in conflict—soldiers and civilians. As a result, questions have arisen as to whether the journalist should be protected as an innocent bystander or, in fact, a willing participant in the military's purposes. Civilians can be innocent bystanders but may also be used as human shields by opposing force. Conversely, journalist are not like civilians in that journalist do not run away but toward a conflict situation. But, they are also unlike military personnel because the journalist is not a combatant in the conflict. This confusion over how to categorize the journalist has led to much debate in the international community with regard to how journalists should be protected by international humanitarian law.

Joanne M. Lisosky and Jennifer Henrichsen,
War on Words: Who Should Protect Journalists?, 2011.

they died. Local journalists and members of news gathering teams are at a disadvantage compared to international correspondents who can easily board an airplane and fly away after the story is done. Yet very little attention is focused on the plight of local journalists covering armed conflict.

International Humanitarian Law

A journalist on a dangerous professional assignment in a conflict area is a civilian and is entitled to all rights granted civilians per se. The Geneva Conventions of 1949 and the two Protocols of 1977 guarantee these rights provided the journalist "does not undertake any action which could jeopardize his civilian status."

Knowing the law may spell the difference between getting killed and staying alive. Surviving and effectively working in a conflict area depends to a large extent on journalists' knowledge and understanding of how the law protects both them and victims of conflict or when the law is being violated.

International humanitarian law, developed to protect in times of conflict persons who do not take part in the hostilities and to limit the violence in achieving military gains, exists in the Geneva Conventions of 1949 and their Additional Protocols of 1977 and other related conventions and treaties.

Under the Geneva Conventions and their Additional Protocols, "civilians are protected from harm. Additional Protocol I, for example, states that in order to ensure respect for, and protection of, the civilian population and civilian property, those fighting must at all times distinguish between the civilian population and combatants and between civilian property and military objectives."

According to [humanitarian law consultant] David Lloyd Roberts, who wrote the Safety and Security Guidelines for Humanitarian Volunteers in Conflict Areas, ". . . the Statute of the International Criminal Court makes it a war crime to carry out intentional attacks against the civilian population or against individual civilians not taking a direct part in hostilities."

As [civilians], journalists do not enjoy special status apart from those provided by law respecting and protecting the rights of civilian populations.

Again, because of the demands and nature of their profession, journalists are lumped under an ill-defined category of people who either closely follow or "embed" with armed forces without necessarily being part of these forces.

Practial Ways to Protect Oneself

Journalists operating with military units in the frontlines run the risk of getting hurt or killed either by the attack of an opposing armed force or by so-called friendly fire. The law offers no protection because rockets fired by an airplane on an armored vehicle on which a journalist is riding cannot stop in mid-flight and say, "hey, there's a reporter on that tank, I better look for another target." Journalists may not lose their right to protection as civilians but de facto protection if they stay too close to a military unit in an operational area.

Aside from the law, there are practical ways by which journalists can protect themselves while operating in hostile environments. The International News Safety Institute, formed in 2003 by the IFJ, International Press Institute, and news organizations like the BBC, recommends safety training and raising awareness among journalists and media staff worldwide. It also provides support and develops safety assistance programs for journalists and freelance staff especially in areas of conflict.

With the world becoming ever more dangerous for journalists and access to conflict zones increasingly denied the media for independent and comprehensive reporting, the fate, in the words of Alain Modoux, "of thousands and even millions of human beings, theoretically protected by the Geneva Conventions, is thus abandoned to the arbitrary decisions of the belligerents, who can act with full impunity, unobserved by embarrassing witnesses."

For journalists to continue being witnesses while staying safe, it is obvious that a complete knowledge as possible of the Geneva Conventions, the Additional Protocols, other treaties and conventions is an absolute must. Knowledge is one of the most powerful weapons that journalists can have in their reporting arsenal. It can, one day, even save their lives.

Periodical and Internet Sources Bibliography

The following articles have been selected to supplement the diverse views presented in this chapter.

Ben Adler	"Why Journalists Aren't Standing Up for WikiLeaks," *Newsweek*, January 4, 2011.
Kim Barker	"Journalism at Risk," *Los Angeles Times*, May 24, 2011.
Matthew Cooper	"Why a Media Shield Law Isn't Enough to Save Journalists," *National Journal*, May 29, 2013.
Glenn Greenwald	"Why Do Journalists Expect to Have Credibility?," *Salon*, March 7, 2010. www.salon.com.
Laura Katherine Layton	"Defining 'Journalist': Whether and How a Federal Reporter's Shield Law Should Apply to Bloggers," *National Law Review*, March 16, 2011.
Rodney Sieh	"Jailed for Journalism," *New York Times*, August 30, 2013.
John Stearns and Chris Palmer	"The Journalism Shield Law: How We Got Here," *Free Press Blog*, August 6, 2013. www.freepress.net/blog.
Jason Stverak	"First Amendment Protects Bloggers, Too," *Washington Examiner*, February 16, 2012.
Jesslyn Tenhouse	"Three J-School Alumni Share How They Defend and Promote First Amendment Freedoms Through Their Careers," *J-School Magazine*, January 2012.
Amy Schmitz Weiss and Cindy Royal	"At the Intersection of Journalism, Data Science, and Digital Media: How Can J-Schools Prep Students for the World They're Headed Into?," Nieman Journalism Lab, July 26, 2013. www.niemanlab.org.

What Is the Future of Journalism?

Chapter Preface

The BBC Academy, the British Broadcasting Corporation's center for training, offers smartphone training for reporters and journalists. "High-end, purpose-built devices undoubtedly give better results, but in the current financial climate the BBC can't give each and every journalist their own portable digital audio recorder, laptop, video camera, stills camera etc.," states Marc Settle, who teaches smartphone reporting at the academy. He also acknowledges that professional equipment can be a hassle to transport and is not always available, unlike ubiquitous handheld devices. "Neither would many of them want to carry a bag containing all of those around with them all the time. Nor are there enough radio cars and satellite trucks to go around. But they do carry their smartphones with them all the time—just like you do, in all likelihood," Settle explains.[1]

Just one day after taking the course, broadcast journalist Stephen Fairclough was on the scene of a stabbing—and the only reporter there. He used his iPhone to cover the story for BBC Wales. "As soon as I arrived, I used the phone to film some short bursts of video. It was dark but the street lights, police floodlights, reflective clothing and white boiler suits of the scenes of crime officers showed up well," Fairclough recollects. "I emailed still pictures back to the newsroom so they could visualise the scene and use the pictures online." He also recorded a voice piece for radio with an app on his smartphone. Without it, Fairclough says that "all I would have been able to do was talk on the phone."[2]

1. Marc Settle, "Smartphones for News: How the Academy Is Helping Journalists Get More Mobile than Ever," BBC. www.bbc.co.uk/academy/news/article/art201307111 64645373.
2. Quoted in Settle, "Smartphones for News."

However, according to Elana Zak, a social media producer at the *Wall Street Journal*, the smartphone cannot replace everything in a reporter's tool kit. For instance, she insists that having a pen and paper is essential even though there are convenient apps for typing and recording. "That won't matter when you're covering the trial of the century in a court house that doesn't allow electronic devices in the building. Or when your iPhone's battery dies at an inopportune moment, say in the middle of an important interview," Zak observes. Moreover, she admits that a printer or copy machine will always come in handy. "Sometimes, there's just no way around needing physical copies of documents," she says, adding that some sources may not be comfortable with digital technology or operate a paperless office. "The only way to get that death certificate or court filing is to print or copy it,"[3] she explains. While technology will no doubt affect the future of journalism, other glimpses of the future of the industry are offered by the authors in this chapter.

3. Elana Zak, "5 Things a Smartphone Can't Replace for a Journalist," 10,000 Words, August 29, 2011. www.mediabistro.com/10000words/5-things-a-smartphone-cant-replace-for-a-journalist_b6372.

| "The trends are clear: people, especially the young, are turning to the Internet for more and more of their news."

The Internet Is Transforming Journalism

Paul Grabowicz

In the following viewpoint, Paul Grabowicz describes how the increasing consumption of news online is changing journalism and challenging news organizations to retain and attract audiences. He contends that many news organizations have adopted a "Web-first" model of publishing, in which content is created for the Internet first. Grabowicz concludes that news organizations now embrace blogging and social networks to connect with audiences and gather news in innovative ways. Paul Grabowicz is senior lecturer, associate dean, and director of the new media program at the University of California–Berkeley's School of Journalism.

As you read, consider the following questions:

1. According to Grabowicz, from what is web-first publishing a major shift?

Paul Grabowicz, "The Transition to Digital Journalism," KDMC Berkeley, June 9, 2013.

2. What did Web 2.0 mean for news organizations, according to the author?

3. How does Grabowicz describe blog postings?

As more people consume news online, news organizations face the dilemma of reallocating resources to attract new readers and viewers while still trying to hold on to their existing, and usually aging, print or broadcast audiences.

Online revenues for most news media are still a small fraction of the income from traditional print or broadcast. And after many years of double-digit annual increases in online advertising revenue, the trend tapered off dramatically in 2008 and 2009, with online revenues flat or even decreasing.

For newspapers, typically 10 percent or less of total revenues come from online operations (although the *Los Angeles Times* reported in late 2008 that online income was enough to pay for the paper's entire print and online news staffs).

Magazines similarly get less than 10 percent of their revenue from their digital operations according to an *Advertising Age* survey of 2008 revenues.

Financial viability for newspapers and most magazines, at least for now, requires retaining as many existing print readers as possible.

Yet the trends are clear: people, especially the young, are turning to the Internet for more and more of their news. . . .

While the trend toward online is clear, the shift has tapered off in recent years. As of the end of 2007, about 25 percent of people in the U.S. still said they hadn't ever been online.

For print and broadcast organizations, this means a core group of their audience remains wedded to traditional products and often resistant to getting news online. . . .

Web-First Publishing

Some newspapers and other news operations are now adopting a "web-first" or "web-centric" approach to organizing their work flow. This means having reporters and editors think first about reporting and producing text and multimedia stories for the web, then writing a text story for the print edition.

This also is sometimes referred to as "reverse publishing."

It marks a major shift from the old "shovelware" approach of newspapers in the 1990s, in which stories were written first for the newspaper and then shoveled onto the web, often with few, if any, changes.

Then in the early 2000s "convergence" strategies started to gain traction at some media organizations, with newspapers, TV stations and radio stations partnering to produce content for a website. But producing stories for the traditional news or broadcast products usually still had top priority.

TBO.com, a partnership of *The Tampa Tribune* and WFLA-TV Channel 8 launched in 2000, was one of the early examples of this move toward convergence. . . .

In 2008, *The Tampa Tribune* moved toward a web-first approach.

"People need to stop looking at TBO.com as an add on to *The Tampa Tribune*. The truth is that *The Tampa Tribune* is an add on to TBO," *Tribune* Managing Editor Janet Coats said in July 2008.

In a web-first approach, the main focus often is on breaking news and getting those stories on the web as fast as possible, on a 24-hour-a-day, 7-days-a-week news cycle.

Some publications have set up "continuous news desks" with dedicated staffs that produce round-the-clock breaking news for the web. *The New York Times* and *Washington Post*, for example, have continuous news desks. . . .

Other publications have emphasized getting all reporters and editors to focus on putting breaking news and other stories on the web, rather than having a separate staff handle story updates for the Internet edition.

In these cases, the publications usually must undergo major reorganizations of their newsrooms and try to train most or all of their editorial staff in writing for the web and producing multimedia. . . .

Web 2.0 and the Rise of Social Media

The concept of Web 2.0 surfaced in the wake of the dot.com crash of 2001 and discussions about what defined companies that were still prospering during the shake-out.

The term was first used in 2004 by Dale Dougherty [vice president of O'Reilly Publishing] in conversations with Tim O'Reilly of O'Reilly Publishing, John Battelle, author of the 2005 book *The Search*, people from MediaLive International that puts on trade shows, and others about planning a conference on the Internet. That led to the Web 2.0 Summit, an annual conference that began in Fall 2004.

In general, Web 2.0 represented a shift away from software companies that tried to lock people into using their products and media companies that published static content for a passive audience, toward a digital culture of public participation, re-mixing by individuals of data and information, harnessing the power of collective intelligence and providing services, rather than products.

The rise of weblogs in the early 2000s was perhaps the best example of this emergence of "social media."

For news organizations, Web 2.0 means moving away from using the Internet to draw a passive audience to a static publishing platform, and instead embracing the broader network, where communication, collaboration, interaction and user-created content are paramount.

Practically it means everything from engaging people on blogs, online forums and social networks, to promoting user generated content and providing more personalized content for mobile devices such as cellphones.

Many news organizations are now embracing the Web 2.0 approach. The Bivings Group, in a 2008 survey of the websites of the 100 largest newspapers, found that:

- 58 percent accepted user-generated photos

- 18 percent accepted user-generated videos

- 15 percent accepted user-generated articles

- 75 percent allowed for comments on articles (up from 33 percent in 2007)

- 76 percent provided some form of a "most popular" list of stories, based on what readers were commenting on or emailing or blogging about

- 92 percent allowed readers to tag stories for inclusion on social bookmarking or aggregation sites like delicious or Digg (compared with only 7 percent in 2006)

- 10 percent utilized social networking tools . . .

Comments on News Stories

One of the most basic ways that a news organization can engage people is to provide a way for them to comment on and discuss news stories on the website and postings to staff weblogs.

Newspapers and magazines have long allowed public comment in the form of letters to the editor. But online comments are as much about people communicating and interacting with each other, as they are just reacting to a reporter's story.

They are a way of engaging people in a conversation about the news and recognizing that a story does not end with its publication, but rather is a starting point for generating commentary and contributions by the public.

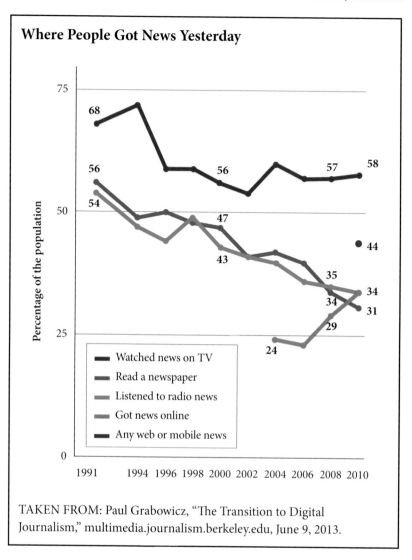

Where People Got News Yesterday

TAKEN FROM: Paul Grabowicz, "The Transition to Digital Journalism," multimedia.journalism.berkeley.edu, June 9, 2013.

But because online comments aren't as strictly vetted as letters to the editor, they have proved vexing for many news organizations.

Only a very small percentage of readers usually will comment on any given news story or blog posting, and most comments will be made by a relative handful of frequent posters who may not be representative of general readership. This has been referred to as the 90–9–1 rule, which means 90 percent of people won't post any comments, 9 percent will post infrequently, and 1 percent will account for the vast majority of the postings. . . .

One survey by *AdAge* found that 63% of readers said they were not more likely to visit a news site because it allowed posting of comments (although young adults were much more inclined to visit sites with commenting).

A few people also will post comments that are offensive or disruptive, quickly turning an intelligent discussion into an online food fight. In the blogging community, such posters are referred to as "trolls."

Another major problem is spammers, who will bombard comments with messages that hawk products or promote online scams.

Because of the offensive postings, a number of news organizations have closed down comments—either temporarily or permanently—after the discussions degenerated into name calling or worse. The *Washington Post*, for example, shut down comments on its post.com blog in January 2006.

As Jim Brady, executive editor of washingtonpost.com, explained the decision:

". . . there are things that we said we would not allow, including personal attacks, the use of profanity and hate speech. Because a significant number of folks who have posted in this blog have refused to follow any of those relatively simple rules, we've decided not to allow comments for the time being." . . .

News organizations also feel the nasty and offensive comments threaten their brands as reputable sources of news.

Some have argued that news organizations just need to swallow hard and live with offensive comments because the value of opening up to reader comments outweighs the downsides. . . .

Journalism and Blogging

News organizations initially were very reluctant to have their reporters or editors set up weblogs, and many viewed bloggers with suspicion or contempt. Bloggers were derided as "pajama-clad" amateurs writing late at night from the comfort of their bedrooms or basements, or "parasites" who did no original reporting and instead were just pundits feasting on the reporting labors of traditional media organizations.

But some news organizations embraced blogging early on, with blogs written by columnists, editors or reporters, often on technology beats. . . .

As blogs gained widespread public adoption in the mid 2000s, more and more media companies embraced them. Columnists and reporters set up personal blogs, usually on their beats, and some news organizations began hosting blogs by members of the public or linking to popular blogs in their coverage areas. . . .

Despite the now widespread acceptance of blogging by news organizations, tensions remain over the role a journalist should play as a blogger and how news organizations should handle their staff-produced blogs.

Most successful bloggers have their own voice or point of view. That's fine for a columnist who starts blogging, but it can be at odds with the traditional media definition of the objective, impartial reporter.

Blog postings are usually not polished editorial products, like a heavily edited story, and a premium is put on doing frequent postings, especially on breaking news. The demands of individual blogging thus can clash with editing and fact-checking functions of news organizations.

News organizations have responded by adopting standards for postings by their in-house staff bloggers. Some publications require that blog posts be edited before being made public, while others allow a reporter to go public with a posting, and then have editors review the postings afterward.

Blogging is not for everyone. Some reporters take to it with enthusiasm, but forcing reluctant reporters to blog is usually a recipe for boring blogs and a demoralized staff.

For reporters who like blogging, it can be an invaluable form of personal branding—establishing themselves in an on-line community, connecting and engaging with the public, getting feedback and story ideas, and participating in the larger conversations going on all over the Internet. . . .

RSS—Syndicating Content

RSS, which stands for Really Simple Syndication, is just that—a very easy way to distribute news content to people, rather than requiring them to visit a news website.

RSS software, created in 1999, lets a website set up a feed of its content such as news stories that people can download and read using an application called an RSS Reader.

The reader can be a software application a person installs on their computer, such as NetNewsWire for Mac computers and FeedDemon for Windows machines.

Or a person can sign up to use a reader hosted on a web-site, such as Google Reader or My Yahoo!

RSS feeds also are a way to distribute your audio or video to mobile devices like the iPod or iPod Touch.

News organizations increasingly are offering RSS feeds of their news stories. . . .

Aggregation Sites

Rather than having professional editors at news organizations determine the important stories of the day, people are taking on this role themselves at aggregation sites where users select and share what they deem the most important news or web-sites.

Users submit stories or websites to be listed on the aggre-gation sites, and other users then vote on or help rank the im-portance of the stories or sites and how prominently they should be displayed.

Examples of aggregators include:

- Reddit—a news stories aggregator that was purchased in 2006 by magazine publisher Condé Nast.

- Mixx—Their motto: "So why should some faceless editor get to decide what's important? But now you're in charge. You find it; we'll Mixx it."

- Delicious—people submit bookmarks of their favorite websites to share them with others. The bookmarks are arranged topically and are ranked by the most popular submissions. You also can find the personal bookmarks of the person who posted them.

- Digg—a news stories aggregator, at which a vote for a story is called a "digg" (Digg was sold in 2012 and is being relaunched as a different service).

- StumbleUpon—another site for sharing favorite websites.

- Publish2—this site is designed for news organizations that want their journalists to share links on news stories and have those links aggregated on the publication's website.

Aggregators also have widgets people can use to embed story feeds on their blogs, websites or personal pages on social networks.

And news websites can place icons for the aggregation services at the end of stories, so readers can click on the icons to submit the stories for inclusion in the listings by the aggregators. . . .

Journalism and Social Networks

For journalists and news organizations, social networks provide an opportunity for connecting with people, distributing news stories and complementing news coverage with feeds from social media.

- Reporters can join the networks, converse with people and showcase their stories. It's yet another way for reporters to develop personal brands for their work.

- News organizations can create their own pages on social networks, such as a fan page on Facebook, and use that to alert people to important news stories the news organization has published or post other items of interest to its followers. Or they can set up their own social networks, using third-party software like Ning or their own homegrown platforms.

- Social networks are great for generating conversations among people about stories. Many news media have found that the volume of reader comments on a story posted on Facebook can exceed comments posted on the news organization's website.

- News organizations can develop widgets that provide feeds of news stories that can be displayed on the personal pages of social network members. . . .

- News sites can use an application like Storify to pull together postings to Facebook, Twitter and other social media sites on a particular topic in the news, especially a breaking news story.

- News media can tell first-person stories using Facebook postings, such as the *Washington Post*'s "A Facebook story: A mother's joy and a family's sorrow," which published a mother's Facebook postings about giving birth and her subsequent medical complications. . . .

- Journalists also can use social networks like Facebook to find sources for stories. . . . For example Facebook's Graph Search . . . can be used to locate people who work at particular companies or organizations, live in specific towns or cities or have particular interests. You also can create Interest Lists in Facebook to create a custom feed of postings by people around specific topics.

Social Networks as a Source of News

People are increasingly learning about news stories via social networks, but the percentage is still small. Only 27 percent of American adults regularly or sometimes get news or news headlines through social networking sites, according to a report by the Pew Research Center released in September 2011. The number increased to 38 percent for people under 30.

During the 2012 presidential primary elections, only 20 percent of people regularly or sometimes got campaign information from Facebook and only 5 percent from Twitter, according to a Pew Research Center survey in February 2012.

A survey by the Reynolds Journalism Institute found that nearly 63 percent of people surveyed said they prefer news stories produced by professional journalists, while less than 21 percent said they prefer to get most of their news from friends they trust.

But Facebook is more popular as a news source among younger people.

Among people 18 to 29 years old, 52 percent get news from Facebook, the top news source for the young, according to a USC Annenberg/*Los Angeles Times* poll in 2012. That compares with 25 percent of people overall who get news from Facebook

| "As media organizations plot their future, it's worth discarding some misconceptions about what it will take to keep the press from becoming yesterday's news."

Myths About the Internet's Transformation of Journalism

Tom Rosenstiel

In the following viewpoint, Tom Rosenstiel identifies five common myths about the Internet's impact on journalism. He notes that one myth is that newspapers are declining around the world, but he contends that the number of newspapers is actually growing. He recommends that media organizations ignore the myths and focus on the facts. Tom Rosenstiel is executive director of the American Press Institute, a nonprofit educational organization that helps the news media advance in the digital age. He is also coauthor of the book Blur: How to Know What's True in the Age of Information Overload.

As you read, consider the following questions:

1. What examples does Rosenstiel provide to support his position that traditional news media are not losing audiences?

2. What is key for media to prosper in the twenty-first century, according to the author?

3. What does Rosenstiel say is the problem with hyperlocal content?

There are few things journalists like to discuss more than, well, themselves and the long-term prospects for their industry. How long will print newspapers survive? Are news aggregation sites the future? Or are online paywalls—such as the one the *New York Times* just launched—the way to go? As media organizations plot their future, it's worth discarding some misconceptions about what it will take to keep the press from becoming yesterday's news.

1. The Traditional News Media are Losing Their Audience.

Many predicted that the rise of the Internet and online publishing meant that mainstream media organizations would lose their readers and viewers, with technology breaking their oligarchic control over news. But that's not the overall picture.

Yes, people are migrating online. In 2010, the Internet passed newspapers for the first time as the platform where Americans "regularly" get news, according to survey data from the Pew Research Center. Forty-six percent of adults say they go online for news at least three times a week, as opposed to 40 percent who read newspapers that often. Only local television news is a more popular destination, at 50 percent.

But online news consumers are heading primarily to traditional sources. Of the 25 most popular news Web sites in the United States, for instance, all but two are "legacy" media sources, such as the *New York Times* or CNN, or aggregators of traditional media, such as Yahoo! or Google News. Of the roughly 200 news sites with the highest traffic, 81 percent are traditional media or aggregators of it. And some old media are seeing their overall audience—in print and on the Web—grow.

The crisis facing traditional media is about revenue, not audience. And in that crisis, newspapers have been hardest hit: Ad revenue for U.S. newspapers fell 48 percent from 2006 to 2010.

2. Online News Will Be Fine as Soon as the Advertising Revenue Catches Up.

Such hopes are misplaced. In 2010, Web advertising in the United States surpassed print advertising for the first time, reaching $26 billion. But only a small fraction of that, perhaps less than a fifth, went to news organizations. The largest share, roughly half, went to search engines, primarily Google. The newspaper industry illustrates the problem. Even though about half the audience may now be accessing papers online, the newspaper industry took in $22.8 billion last year in print ad revenue but only $3 billion in Web-based revenue.

Journalism thrived in decades past because news media were the primary means by which industry reached customers. In the new media landscape, there are many ways to reach the audience, and news represents only a small share.

3. Content Will Always Be King.

The syllogism that helped journalism prosper in the 20th century was simple: Produce the journalism (or "content") that people want, and you will succeed. But that may no longer be enough.

The key to media in the 21st century may be who has the most knowledge of audience behavior, not who produces the most popular content. Understanding what sites people visit, what content they view, what products they buy and even their geographic coordinates will allow advertisers to better

Speeding Up the Circulation of Fabrication

In an age of revolutionary technology, the weakening of editorial practices and the devaluing of truth make it easier not only for unsubstantiated news stories to speedily gain widespread circulation but also for technically deft, media-savvy hucksters to sell their fabrications as truth to reporters, and by extension to the public. Such fabrications are sometimes pranks, motivated by a simple desire to hoodwink a press that is endlessly hungry for sensation and attention. But fabrications also have played more serious and well-documented roles in recent times in efforts to undermine a candidate's drive for his party's presidential nomination with a digitally tricked-up photograph, to damage a president's reelection campaign with digitally invented military service records, and even to provide false evidence of a clear and present danger justifying the decision to launch a war against another nation.

Neil Henry, American Carnival: Journalism Under Siege in an Age of New Media, *2007.*

target individual consumers. And more of that knowledge will reside with technology companies than with content producers.

Google, for instance, will know much more about each user than will the proprietor of any one news site. It can track users' online behavior through its Droid software on mobile phones, its Google Chrome Web browser, its search engine and its new tablet software.

The ability to target users is why Apple wants to control the audience data that goes through the iPad. And the company that may come to know the most about you is Facebook, with which users freely share what they like, where they go and who their friends are.

4. Newspapers Around the World Are on the Decline.

Actually, print circulation worldwide was up more than 5 percent in the past five years, and the number of newspapers is growing. In general, print media are thriving in the developing world and suffering in rich nations. Print newspaper ad revenue, for instance, rose by 13 percent in India and by 10 percent in Egypt and Lebanon in the last year for which data is available. But it fell by 8 percent in France and 20 percent in Japan.

The forces tied to a thriving print newspaper industry include growing literacy, expanding population, economic development and low broadband penetration. In India, for example, the population is growing and becoming more literate, but a substantial portion is not yet online.

By and large, American newspapers are suffering the most. Roughly 75 percent of their revenue comes from advertising, vs. 30 percent or 40 percent in many other countries, where papers live and die by circulation. That means the collapse of advertising is not hitting papers elsewhere as hard as it is hitting them here. It also suggests that the need to charge for online access may be even more important abroad.

5. The Solution Is to Focus on Local News.

Going "hyperlocal" was the war cry of Wall Street to the news industry five years ago [in 2006]. The reasoning was simple: In the Internet age, when users can access content from anywhere, it didn't make sense for local operations to compete with the big national news providers.

The problem is that hyperlocal content, by definition, has limited appeal. To amass an audience large enough to generate significant ad revenue, you have to produce a large volume of content from different places, and that is expensive. On top of that, many hyperlocal advertisers are not yet online, limiting the ad dollars.

Now we are entering what might be called Hyperlocal 2.0, and the market is still up for grabs. Google, which garners two-thirds of all search advertising dollars nationally, doesn't exert similar control over local advertising. Locally, display ads—all those banners and pop-ups—are a bigger share of the market than search ads.

But how to produce local content remains a mystery. Can you put paywalls around it? Can you build a "pro-am" model, in which professional journalists work with low-paid amateurs to produce a comprehensive report? Or will the winner be something like AOL's Patch, in which hundreds of hyperlocal sites are owned by a single company that can connect those readers with major advertisers?

So far, no one has really cracked the code for producing profitable local news online.

| "No one seems to believe that a revival
of print circulation is still possible."

Newspapers Will
Become Obsolete

Richard J. Tofel

In the following viewpoint, Richard J. Tofel claims that newspapers are disappearing because they gave away their content on the Internet for free. He maintains that the dominance of newspapers has come to an end, and if they survive at all, they will be much less profitable. Tofel asserts that, nevertheless, it is the continuation of quality journalism that matters. Richard J. Tofel is the general manager of the nonprofit news agency ProPublica.

As you read, consider the following questions:

1. Why is the fall of newspapers in 2005 especially jarring, according to Tofel?

2. What does the author say the loss of newspapers means to him?

3. How has newspapers' competition changed since 1995, according to Tofel?

The business model that had fueled the golden age of American newspapers broke somewhere around 2005. Total advertising revenues began dropping, and, at least at this writing [2012], it seems unlikely they will rise appreciably again, at least until print newspapers have literally disappeared and been replaced by some digital future that is still emerging. Print circulation levels—the number of copies sold—continued a swoon that went back decades and now seems almost certain to be terminal. Costs were cut everywhere they could be—buyouts and layoffs of employees, fewer pages, smaller pages—but the cost cuts could not keep up with the revenue declines, and profits tumbled. The most heavily leveraged newspapers—in Los Angeles, Chicago, Philadelphia, Minneapolis, St. Louis, and elsewhere—ended up in bankruptcy while those saddled with lower debt limped along, some still profitable, many of the best—in Washington and Boston, for instance—not.

It was quite a fall, most jarring for at least two reasons. First, the most profitable year in the history of American newspapers had come in the year 2000, a very recent memory. If the internet killed newspapers, it had hardly done so in "internet time." Next, the breakdown of the newspaper business model was most confusing because newspaper audiences were still growing, and larger than ever before. Print circulation declines were greatly exceeded by the growth in the newspapers' online audience. One promise of the digital future—that audiences not limited by distance or eventually even by language could be served instantaneously, with the cost of serving the marginal reader reduced to zero—had been fully realized. On the day when the *Los Angeles Times*'s parent company filed for bankruptcy, the *Times* enjoyed a larger audience for its news than ever before. Ditto for the *Washington Post* on the day it slid from profitability to unprofitability. And the audiences continued to grow as the bankruptcies lengthened and the losses ballooned. But, of course, print customers paid for their copies and digital readers generally did not. . . .

Moving in Another Direction

Newspaper publishers initially seemed to be moving in another direction. In April 1995 eight of the largest newspaper companies (not including the parents of the *New York Times* or the *Wall Street Journal*, but collectively owning 185 newspapers with a combined Sunday circulation of 23 million) announced they had formed a consortium they dubbed the New Century Network. It was intended to forge common standards and tools for metropolitan newspapers in launching paid sites on the web. The New York Times Company joined New Century a month later. But New Century did not even launch for two years, burning through much of the initial capital contributions of a million dollars from each member company while the first 18 months were spent in part searching for a permanent CEO [chief executive officer] for the venture and debating whether to take it public in a partnership with [venture capital firm] Kleiner Perkins. By then, New Century had simply been overtaken by events as member newspapers launched their own sites—nearly all of them free. (New Century launched what amounted to a portal in April 1997. It shut down in March 1998 after spending $25 million.)

Free to the Web

Meanwhile the *Wall Street Journal*, excluded from New Century because its parent company owned the Dow Jones news wire, offered a free version of its core Money & Investing section on the web in mid-1995; *USA Today* followed with a free version of its entire paper in August, just as Microsoft launched its competition with Netscape. The *Boston Globe* came free to the web in October 1995, and the *New York Times* in January 1996. The online magazine *Salon* began publication as a free product in November 1995. . . .

The *San Jose Mercury News*, capitalizing on the rise of Silicon Valley to contend for a place as one of the country's leading newspapers, had begun offering what it called Mercury Center on AOL in May 1993 (when AOL had just 250,000 members), and had begun testing a web version of Mercury Center in December 1994. By July 1996, even though AOL membership had grown to six million, Mercury Center left AOL to concentrate on its web future. In May 1998 it became a free site.

The *Wall Street Journal* launched a full web version in April 1996 and said free access would last only through July. That deadline was postponed three times, and a special deal was struck with Microsoft to offer Internet Explorer users free access through the end of the year; but the *Journal* converted to a paid site by the beginning of 1997, losing nearly 90 percent of its online audience in the process. Soon, among major newspapers, it was the only one that had made this choice. At the time it was said that the *Journal* had left the future behind. Alternatively, some said a business newspaper was somehow different, possibly because companies rather than individuals paid for readers' subscriptions—a phenomenon that had actually largely ended in the 1980s. Much later (particularly when the *Journal* adapted to the prevalence of search by making all its content freely accessible via search results), its perhaps $100 million in annual digital circulation revenue became the envy of the industry, though, to be sure, even the *Journal* was only marginally profitable.

The Culture of Newspapers

How did this happen? Why? What happened, particularly in 1995 and 1996, that convinced nearly all newspaper publishers to give away their content on the internet?

And why does it matter? What difference did it make?

The latter questions seem to me easier to answer. It matters for two reasons. First, because of the old saw about the need to understand history if we are to avoid the doom that can come with repeating it. And it makes a difference because the loss of newspapers is a loss to no less than our democracy, to the capacity of our people for self-government. Not that new news sources have not arisen, and will not continue to arise. They have and will; I have poured the last four years of my working life into creating one of them. But the loss to democratic governance is greater than the gains we have made, and seems likely to remain so.

Which brings us back to the first question: How did this happen?

How, as a visitor from another planet might ask, did a large industry that had successfully charged customers for its product for more than a century come to decide to give that product away and thus threaten its very existence? The answer can be found on any number of levels, though I think it ultimately lies in an understanding of the culture of newspapers and newspapering.

The late 1990s were boom years for the national economy, and the technology revolutions were an important element of the boom. At the close of 1982 *Time* magazine had named the computer the "Machine of the Year," but personal computers first passed 50 percent penetration in homes with incomes above $50,000 only in May 1994. The release of Windows '95 was seen as a significant societal moment. Netscape went public in August 1995 with a market capitalization that instantly rose to nearly $3 billion—more than that of the New York Times Company—and visions of digital-division IPO [initial public offering] sugarplums were dancing in the heads of many executives. By April 1997 the four leading online services had a collective sixteen million members. The advertising business, always taken with the latest thing, was thrilled with even the most primitive forms of online creative. *Wired* reported that standard advertising rates in April 1996 were $15 per thousand impressions (occasions when a particular ad is downloaded)—between four and ten times prevailing rates today in constant dollars. At a time when some political theorists talked seriously of an "end of history," a few economic observers speculated that technological change might have fundamentally altered the very notion of business cycles.

The Business Model Broke for Good

Such thinking may have played an important role in supporting thinking about the best business model for newspapers in the new online world.

Traditionally, advertising was the engine of newspaper profitability, the largest source of newspaper revenue and the key determinant of whether years were good or less good. Circulation revenue was not as important—in many cases only half as large as advertising. But while advertising was cyclical, rising and falling largely in sync with the macroeconomy, circulation tended to be steadier. The consequence was that, in recession years, circulation revenue held up while advertising fell. And in such years, circulation made the difference between newspapers showing smaller profits instead of falling into losses. Of course, if recessions (like strategic military threats) were a thing of the past, this did not matter as much.

Things didn't work out that way. The internet has hardly repealed the economic cycle—we are just now emerging from the second contraction since the invention of the web browser. The year the internet stock bubble burst, 2000, was also the year of peak newspaper profitability.

Nor has the digital age transformed the ancient laws of supply and demand. In about 2005 a number of phenomena, including higher broadband penetration, the ubiquity of search, the beginning of the rise of social media, the proliferation of blogs, and easier-to-use web publishing tools all combined to create an explosion in the quantity of pages on which web advertising could be placed. (Today, Facebook alone accounts for perhaps one in four web pages viewed online.) As a result, the price of advertising on any of those pages fell pre-cipitously, and nearly all publishers found themselves with enormous quantities of unsold online advertising. Right about then was when the newspaper business model broke for good. Growing competition for readers' time (and shrinking atten-tion spans) was eroding usage of the print product while the revenue potential of digital versions was collapsing. Advertis-ing spending had been placed under great pressure since at least 2001 as new online tools significantly demystified the decades-old question posed by [marketing pioneer] John Wanamaker: Much of the cost of advertising was known to be waste, but which part? Online the answer was known, as user behavior could be carefully tracked; offline it seemed suddenly much more knowable, as advertisers demanded quantification where once anecdotes had sufficed.

A Circular Argument

Some of this was unforeseeable in 1994–1997. ("Social media"?) But much could have been foreseen, and was (broadband, search, blogs, publishing efficiencies, targeted advertising). The truth is that the collapse in online advertis-ing pricing around 2005, after these trends had begun to play out, should have been far less surprising than the artificially high level—the novelty level—of online advertising pricing in 1995.

Yet some in the newspaper industry still maintain that they had no choice ... the word most often employed in this century is "scale," the sheer size needed to operate efficiently and effectively. Without scale, they say, newspapers could never have competed online with other media for advertising at all. Without scale, newspapers would have been vulnerable to alternative purveyors of content, such as the wire services that had long provided news to them but not directly to con-sumers, or CNN and other cable television news upstarts.

There is something to this argument, but not as much as may first meet the eye. The leading wire service in the United States, and the only one that offered a full range of general-interest news and information in the mid-1990s, was the Associated Press [AP], which is actually a cooperative owned by the nation's newspapers. It is the worst form of circular argument to say that newspapers needed to give away their content to rebuff competition from the AP. They could, quite simply, have forbade such competition—refused, for instance, to permit the AP to offer the news that fueled much of the growth of Yahoo! as a news source online. Might Reuters or UPI [United Press International] or CNN have stepped in to play a similar role in partnership with Yahoo!? Perhaps. But at the time Reuters was largely a business wire in this country, and it lacked the capital that would have been required to grow quickly to the sort of size it has achieved these fifteen long years [1997–2012] later. Ditto Bloomberg. CNN? It is always difficult and probably foolhardy to say what [CNN founder] Ted Turner might have done, but CNN is facing challenges today building a text wire, and it is hard to be confident it could have accomplished the task more easily before its acquisition by Time Warner in late 1996.

Giving Away Content

And scale has proven insufficient to save newspapers. By one common measure, the *New York Times* has nearly 60 million unique visitors to its website each month, but the market capitalization of the entire Times Company (including the *Boston Globe* and About.com) hovers near $1 billion, the accepted dividing line between "mid" and "small" capitalization stocks, and the company suspended all dividends to shareholders nearly three years ago [in 2008]. The *Washington Post* and *Los Angeles Times* have about 25 million average monthly uniques, *USA Today* 18 million—probably ten times the maximum readership they enjoyed in the glory days of print—and all are in dire economic straits.

Today it seems clear that the economic future of newspapers depends on their maintaining a near-monopoly on high-quality local news and on achieving a substantial level of circulation revenues, ideally online, (No one seems to believe that a revival of print circulation is still possible.) Newspapers, it is now widely recognized, will generally not be mass media in the truest sense—the sense of network television, Google, and Facebook—but will be smaller players, with products targeted to the higher end of news consumers. Newspaper companies will, if they survive at all, have lower revenues and much lower profit margins than they did a decade ago. Advertising will be only one element of their revenue mix.

If all this is true, it must follow that the decision to give away newspaper content was a mistake, that an alternative future in which nearly all newspapers sought to charge for such content on the web, just as they had charged for it in print and on the online proprietary services, would quite likely have produced a happier outcome.

Important Revenues Lost

Perhaps newspapers would have suffered in any event. Perhaps barriers to the creation of comprehensive packages of local content would have fallen even if newspapers had used digital circulation revenues to augment content and *raise* those barriers, instead of voluntarily lowering them by cutting back on content as print circulation fell and digital distribution produced no circulation revenue at all.

Perhaps the advent of the internet meant that only truly *mass* media, such as broadcast television, were destined to still be able to base profits solely on advertising, and that newspapers were right to try to join the mass-media crowd, even if they had little chance of achieving sustained "scale" for the consumption of their content, of the sort television has long enjoyed. Note, in this connection, that newspapers now talk of how many millions of users come to their sites once a *month*, where broadcast television can still talk of the millions who watch every night. (Of course, the demise of broadcast television at the hands of the internet may yet lie ahead.)

Perhaps. Perhaps not. But there can be little doubt that a collective decision to charge for content would have yielded important revenues in the short term, and, if the decision could have been sustained, might have yielded more such revenue, at least for quality providers, as time went on. . . .

A Hinge Point in History

But we need to conclude on a note of further clarity: to say that a monumental mistake was made in 1995–1996 is *not* a prescription for business models in 2012. Consumers have been accustomed to a cornucopia of free content for nearly a generation now. And the newspaper industry is, in many places, a shadow of what it was in 1995—all those cuts in staff and content have made a difference, eroding the quality, the essentiality, and certainly the uniqueness of what they have to offer. Not only has the internet lowered the barriers to entry; newspapers have voluntarily lowered them as well, precisely when they should have been fighting (and investing) to build such barriers.

Nor have competitors stood still. Where in 1995 there was one quality general news wire in America, now there are three, with both Bloomberg and Reuters in some ways overtaking the Associated Press, especially with respect to the ability to produce differentiating stories, the sort of reporting that has impact, that builds journalistic brands. Where in 1995 there were few if any local news organizations that could compete with newspapers on any level, now, in many communities, such organizations are growing—out of public radio, or local broadcast or cable television, or emerging nonprofits. And both search and social media have profoundly altered the common means of discovery of content, undercutting established brands, or at least putting powerful competitive tools in the hands of upstarts.

This has been a meditation on one of those hinge points in history, not an exercise in nostalgia or a call to somehow repeal the past. The business model of newspapers has been broken, irretrievably I believe, for about seven years now; the roots of that crisis run back a good bit farther, as we have seen. But journalism retains its critical role in our society as no less than the essential enabler of democratic self-government.

As we move past the era of newspapers as the dominant form of journalism, we ought to recall how we got here. But we should also fix our sights on why we care: not because of emotional attachment to a particular business model, or even to journalistic nameplates, the most venerable of which are hardly old, even by the standards of American institutions. (The glory days of the *New York Times* began only in the [President William] McKinley administration [1897–1901], in the 108th year of government under the Constitution. The *Washington Post* and *Wall Street Journal* were still backwaters when the Great Depression began.)

We should care not about newspapers themselves but about the highest level of quality journalism that they have represented for a century or so. The future of that kind of journalism will depend largely on our ability to create new institutions, and adapt old ones, so that we can respond to technological change with business creativity, entrepreneurial determination, self-confidence, and common sense. In short, this time we need to do better.

| "*The print version of newspapers must find its own way to survive, and I believe it will.*"

Newspapers Will Survive

Alex S. Jones

In the following viewpoint, Alex S. Jones argues that newspapers can survive the sweeping changes brought about by the Internet. He maintains that print and Internet products must be managed separately in this transitional stage. He concludes that newspapers must publish news that is innovative, provocative, and indispensable if they are to survive. Alex S. Jones is a Pulitzer Prize–winning journalist and the director of the Shorenstein Center on Media, Politics, and Public Policy, a research center at Harvard University. This viewpoint is excerpted from his book, Losing the News: The Future of the News That Feeds Democracy.

As you read, consider the following questions:

1. How does the newspaper industry compare with the railroad industry, according to Jones?

2. Who are the journalists of the future, in the author's opinion?

3. What concept does Jones say the leading newspapers on the Internet have grasped?

There is a great deal that powerful people and institutions seek to keep hidden, and far more that would be hidden were it not for the vigilance of a watchdog press corps. Indeed, far too much goes unwatched and unreported as it is; the act of saving the news should, in fact, include a goad and a prod to news organizations to be more rigorous. While Web-based organizations can break news, it has been the best newspapers that have done the deep reporting. In this time of transition, when so much is unclear and uncertain about the future of news, there are reasons to be hopeful and—even more important—there are actions to be taken. But there isn't much time.

To roam the Web is to wander in a world so dazzling in its breadth and innovation that there is a kind of vertigo of head-shaking wonder at the speed with which it has changed our world. No one can doubt that the world of the future is going to be centered on the Web and digital technology, and that saving the news has to begin by recognizing that. This does not mean that there will be no printed news or books, but the world has already changed for most Americans into one that *requires* interaction online, and that requirement will only increase. Saving the news in no way means damming up the current that is running so very strong. The current can sweep away everything in its path, or it can be guided like a river shaped by levees so that it irrigates the land instead of destroying it. The market doesn't care where the Web goes, as long as it results in profit. I have lost any illusion I may have had that the market is always the wisest arbiter, and I think that in the case of news, a purely market-driven future will damage or even destroy the iron core.

A Commercial Core

That said, I also believe that an enduring solution for preserving the iron core of news and traditional journalism standards has to be a commercial one. Katharine Graham, the legendary publisher and owner of the *Washington Post*, famously observed that the best guarantee of first-class journalism is a strong bottom line. A marginally profitable news organization is too weak to withstand the kind of punishment that comes from publishing news that makes powerful people mad. The more tenuous the news organization financially, the more timid and vulnerable to self-censorship. The Idaho Falls *Post Register* probably could not have taken on the most powerful institutions in its town, and weathered an advertising boycott, without a sound economic foundation. Similarly, a financially successful news organization can afford to pay the wages and health care benefits of the caliber of journalistic talent that is required for serious news reporting. A news organization that is losing money has few choices, and, while hard times can be endured for a while, a business that is chronically only marginally profitable is likely doomed.

I define "saving the news" as finding a commercial model that will sustain professional journalism focused on serious news, conducted with traditional values and standards for a broad audience in towns and cities throughout the nation. This does not necessarily mean saving newspapers, though they remain the greatest source of the kind of accountability journalism I want saved. If newspapers as a species die, that will simply be reality, and we shall have to figure out how to save the news without newspapers. But I have not given up on newspapers, and I think they have a future, if only they can endure long enough to find it. Those who sound the death knell for newspapers liken their plight to that of silent movies when the talkies began to appear. I see them as more like the railroad industry in the face of airplanes, automobiles, and interstate highways. Railroads were forced out of the city-to-city passenger business, which they had once dominated. But the industry survived by hauling freight and now trains move about two-thirds of the total tonnage in the country. Newspapers have to find a way to haul freight.

Downsizing May Be a Blessing

The first challenge for the nation's newspapers is to figure out a way to stay in business in the face of the worst economic downturn since the Depression. Newspapers were already reeling from epochal technological change when the economy collapsed. In December 2008, as it became clear that advertising was falling off a cliff and revenues were plummeting, many newspapers found themselves in a triage situation, killing parts of themselves to keep the rest alive. Cost reduction, which had already cut away much of the fat, now began to slice off muscle and bone. The few remaining cities with competing papers saw the weaker go down, such as the *Rocky Mountain News* in Denver and the *Post-Intelligencer* in Seattle. The *Detroit News* and the *Detroit Free Press* tried a different tack, preserving their reporting strength but eliminating home delivery several days a week. Everywhere, newspapers were demanding concessions and enduring painful layoffs. At our family paper, we had the first layoffs in our history, and it was excruciating. Ultimately, the downsizing may prove to be a blessing in that the industry has to reinvent itself on a lower cost basis if it is to survive, and such wrenching changes tend to happen when extinction is the alternative. The newspaper industry that emerges will be leaner and, when the economy turns and some of the lost advertising returns, the new revenue will have an outsized reviving power like food to a starving man. The result may be a surge in profitability and a chance to face the more daunting challenge of secular change.

A Generational Change

Newspapers are in a situation in which, as my grandmother would say, the rabbit has to climb a tree. But the change is of a magnitude that many newspaper owners have even now not fully grasped. It is not unlike the moment when rock and roll with its pounding rhythms and speed blew away the quieter popular music of Frank Sinatra and Bing Crosby. That was a

generational change. Today, the nation's newspaper newsrooms are largely occupied by people for whom the Web is familiar but not ingrained. They are not trained to be the journalists of the future, who will have to be able to report with
shrewdness, write well, and also have a facility with working
in a 24/7 news environment, shooting videos, creating audio
reports, blogging, interacting with readers and citizen journalists, coming up with dazzling graphics, and adapting to a cas-
cade of ever-newer Web applications so they can create journalism for everything from the print newspaper to cell phone
screens, Web television, and podcasts. Similarly, on the business side the environment is fiercely competitive, and will only
grow more so as Web-based rivals multiply without the barriers to entry that printing presses and broadcast licenses represented. In the 1960s and '70s, family newspaper owners were
undone when printing technology changed and people began
leaving newspapers for television. Those who preferred not to
assume the risk left the business. Compared to the fear and
trauma of what lies ahead for newspapers now, that transition
was simple. This time around, the change is so extreme that
no one really knows what is coming or who will survive.

In November 2008, in the midst of the worst fall for newspapers in memory, 50 senior newspaper executives from most
of the nation's leading newspaper companies gathered behind
closed doors at the American Press Institute outside Washington, D.C., to try to figure out how to save their businesses. It
was billed as a "Summit on Saving an Industry in Crisis," and
the participants listened as people like James Shein, a turn-
around specialist at the Kellogg School of Management at
Northwestern University, led them through the psychological
phases of dealing with a faltering business. First, being blind
to eroding conditions followed by an inaction bred of denial
and finally to "faulty action" in hope of a quick fix, such as
slashing costs by dumping the reporters who are the chief creators of the only product that will potentially save their busi-

nesses. Full-blown crisis is next, followed by "dissolution." It was not a cheery message, and the advice seemed to be essentially to do *something* productive and imaginative, and if that doesn't work to try something else. According to Shein, "Ready, fire, aim" should be the operating principle. Though there was a lot of discussion about research and development and collaboration, the only action taken by the group was to agree to reconvene in six months.

But the hardy newspaper owners who suck it up and move into the future still have some significant advantages. The commercial lesson of the Web—at least so far—has been that established brands have the advantage. The most frequently visited news-generating Web sites belong to CNN and the *New York Times.* Local news organizations are known and familiar, though the trends suggest that this head start may carry them only until competition stiffens. They have a chance, though, to adapt.

Two Businesses Rather than One

So, what should forward-thinking owners of news organizations be doing now? They should recognize that these are hard times unlike anything seen before. They are going to have to spend some serious money, endure smaller profits, and have the faith that the future will reward them. They should start by recognizing that they have two businesses rather than one. The print newspaper is one thing. The Web newspaper, to my mind, must be viewed not as a complementary or ancillary product, but as something utterly different: a separate business and a separate news organization.

This is *not* the way newspaper owners see things, for the most part. They are dealing with the Web by tasking their reporters and ad salesmen to serve both the print and online products, which I believe is a strategy that is unlikely to succeed as the Web picks up speed and sophistication and diverges more and more from the old established media genres.

The Web is going to be a medium of its own. Thinking that a successful hybrid can be manufactured by print journalists and ad salesmen used to selling space and inserts is like asking Sinatra to sing "Blue Suede Shoes." He can do it, after a fashion, but it isn't what he *does*. It isn't his authentic self. Newspapers—the printed ones—have an authenticity that is their greatest strength, and a Web newspaper must have the same. They both reflect a specific culture that needs, in both cases, to be respected. You can't do either on the cheap and get away with it for long. This is a concept that some of the best newspapers have already grasped, and they are infusing their Web sites with a sensibility of their own. Not surprisingly, washingtonpost.com and nytimes.com are leaders in this, using the reporting of the newspaper staff as a point of departure for a new environment that has the multiplatforms of the Web.

A Transitional Stage

But even these sites may not prove to be sufficiently appealing to an audience that is steeped in the culture of the Web, which is faster, more irreverent, more subjective, cruder, more experimental, and geared to an audience with a short attention span. When news sites offer up expansive online databases and scores of links to deepen reporting, they are serving a traditional news sensibility, not the sensibility of the Web. The daunting question then becomes whether traditional news organizations should move so far outside their traditional culture that they have a real chance of capturing the attention of this new Web-centric audience. And if they do, will they have to leave behind the standards of journalism that have been at the heart of their value system? The state of newspaper Web sites now is one that could be considered newspaper-plus, and the sensibility remains, despite a Web presence, very much that of a traditional newspaper.

My sense is that this will prove to be a transitional stage, and the Web will continue to establish its own standards and practices and culture, just as television did. In the 1950s, when TV was young, the style of television news was largely stiff and serious, with radio and print reporters going before the camera. But as time passed, television news developed into a medium with its own style and limits. For instance, in the early days, TV news judgments were similar to those of print, and there were a lot of talking heads. But TV's power came to be recognized as moving pictures. And that realization has evolved into a widely observed principle of television news that if there are no good pictures, TV doesn't do the story. That is why you rarely see a public policy question explored in any depth on TV, and why you see so much junk that has the virtue of great video.

The important point is that each of the traditional forms of media has a culture of its own that needs to be respected, and the traditional way of dealing with news may not lend itself to the Web. National Public Radio (NPR), for example, would not seem an apt prospect for a Web site that tried to offer written news, video, and such. Its Web site will probably be an alternate delivery system, with some interaction, some video, and added bells and whistles that are appropriate. But should NPR try to become both the *New York Times* and ABC News? It does not seem a sensible strategy. Similarly, every news organization will have an alternate delivery system on the Web, with the additions and gizmos that a Web audience now expects. And this will gradually—or perhaps not so gradually—evolve into something quite apart, with an identity that will be more brotherly than complementary, and with a largely separate staff.

The Best Guarantee for Newspapers

This means that the print version of newspapers must find its own way to survive, and I believe it will—or at least that it can. No one really knows what the bottom is in terms of circulation and advertising for newspapers, but there seems every reason to think that it has not yet been reached. The instincts of a lifetime spent in print journalism tell me that the best guarantee of reaching a stable and sustainable level of both advertising and circulation is to publish a newspaper that is strong, brave, and rich in quality and in personality. It should have reporters and editors whose job is to publish the most innovative, most provocative, most interesting news it can find, and trust that readers will find that indispensable.

| "*Investigative reporters are a vanishing species in the forests of dead tree media and missing in action on Action News.*"

Investigative Journalism Is Declining

Mary Walton

In the following viewpoint, Mary Walton contends that investigative journalism—vital to exposing systemic corruption and injustice—is vanishing as budgets and staffs shrink at news organizations across the nation. She explains that the reporters who remain are assigned to several beats and forced to multitask, left with no time or resources to probe into stories. She asserts that nonprofit organizations dedicated to investigative journalism are springing up to fill the void. Mary Walton is a former reporter for the Philadelphia Inquirer *and author of numerous nonfiction books.*

As you read, consider the following questions:

1. What characterized the "golden era" of investigative journalism, according to Walton?

2. What figures does the author cite to estimate the number of investigative journalists at newspapers?

3. According to Walton, what trends regarding prizes and awards support the claim that newspapers are abandoning investigative reporting?

On her last day at Fort Lauderdale's *Sun-Sentinel*, Mc Nelly Torres knew another round of layoffs was in the works. She went out for coffee, came back and said a prayer. The phone rang and a familiar name flashed on the screen. It was the editor they called the "Angel of Death." Earlier in the day, Torres learned she had won a Green Eyeshade Award in consumer reporting from the Society of Professional Journalists, her second in as many years. Now she was out of a job.

Roberta Baskin, director of the investigative team at WJLA, the ABC affiliate in Washington, D.C., was waiting to take the bus back from New York City, where she had collected her third duPont-Columbia Award. Her cell phone rang. It was her news director telling her she had been let go, along with 24 other employees.

Tom Dubocq didn't wait for the ax to fall. At the *Palm Beach Post*, an era of fat budgets was dissolving like lard in a hot frying pan. In a single month in 2008, the staff of roughly 300 was reduced to 170, greased by a buyout offer that included health benefits for life. Dubocq's prize-winning probes of local corruption had put three county commissioners and assorted others in jail. He had his eye on a fourth commissioner, but instead signed up for the buyout. He was, he says, making too much money. "I knew ultimately I would get laid off. It was time to make the move."

What happens, I ask Dubocq, when people like him vanish from the newsrooms of America?

"The bad guys get away with stuff."

A Vanishing Species

Kicked out, bought out or barely hanging on, investigative reporters are a vanishing species in the forests of dead tree media and missing in action on Action News. I-Teams are shrinking or, more often, disappearing altogether. Assigned to cover multiple beats, multitasking backpacking reporters no longer have time to sniff out hidden stories, much less write them. In Washington, bureaus that once did probes have shrunk, closed and consolidated.

The membership of Investigative Reporters and Editors [IRE] fell more than 30 percent, from 5,391 in 2003, to a 10-year low of 3,695 in 2009. (After a vigorous membership drive, this year [2010] the number climbed above 4,000.) Prize-seekers take note: Applications for Pulitzers are down more than 40 percent in some investigative categories, a drop reflected in other competitions.

"There is no question that there are fewer investigative reporters in the U.S. today than there were a few years ago, mirroring the overall loss of journalists at traditional media outlets," says IRE Executive Director Mark Horvit. While he concedes that the situation is alarming, Horvit points to positive developments. New organizations dedicated to investigative and watchdog coverage have sprung up, and some mainstream news outlets are renewing a commitment that had been lost.

In July [2010], a major investigative project underscored the importance of journalists as watchdogs of democracy: the *Washington Post* series "Top Secret America," on the nation's bloated security establishment. Would that more journalists had been on duty when subprime mortgage peddlers were running amok and the federal Minerals Management Service was sitting on a potential oil disaster.

"Eternal vigilance by the people is the price of liberty," [President] Andrew Jackson declared in his 1837 Farewell Address. But what if the people don't know what's going on? "All citizens have a right to petition the government for redress of grievances," former *Newsday* Editor Anthony J. Marro, a one-time investigative reporter and a champion of accountability journalism, told a gathering of the Vermont ACLU [American Civil Liberties Union] last year, "but, as simplistic as it sounds, without a strong press they often don't know what the grievances are."

Elevated to hero status after two *Washington Post* reporters [Carl Bernstein and Bob Woodward] helped bring down a corrupt U.S. president [Richard M. Nixon] and his cronies, investigative reporters enjoyed a golden era from the late 1970s into the 2000s. In cities blessed with activist media, reporters took aim at corruption, waste, incompetence and injustice in politics, government, charities and corporations. Cameras confronted culprits. An aroused populace demanded change. People went to jail; old laws were rewritten and new ones passed. Competition for investigative prizes swelled; others came into being.

The annual conferences of IRE, organized in 1975, were like revival meetings, infusing adherents with new energy and skills, and winning converts to the craft. Big names like Donald L. Barlett and James B. Steele of the *Philadelphia Inquirer* and My Lai[1] hero Seymour Hersh drew rock-star crowds. Newspapers and networks came looking for talent, and reporters came armed with résumés and clips. Free newspapers greeted early morning risers. The conference still draws well, but some of the bells and whistles are silent. At this year's [2010] conference, attended by 800, not even the host—the *Las Vegas Sun*—gave away copies.

Shrinking Media Resources and Rosters

Never has there been a greater need for probing coverage of the multiple ways in which the public is victimized. But as

---

1. My Lai was the site of a massacre of about five hundred Vietnamese civilians by American troops during the Vietnam War in 1968, which was covered up by the US military; Hersh investigated and broke the story in late 1969.

corporations sprawl across continents and government grows more complex, media resources shrink. The year 2008 was brutal for the nation's press. Some 5,900 daily print journalists dropped off the rolls, according to the annual count by the American Society of News Editors. And 2009 wasn't much better. Another 5,200 jobs disappeared. Meanwhile, in 2008 local television news shed 1,200 jobs, a 4.3 percent decline, according to a Radio Television Digital News Association survey. The slide tapered off in 2009; just 400 people lost their jobs. In network news, however, ABC alone cut 400 jobs in March of this year; CBS had already let 70 go.

The shrinking rosters represent a two-front assault on investigative reporting. Investigations take time, lots of time. With much smaller staffs doing much more work in a multimedia era, it becomes harder to spring reporters from their day jobs to tackle important but labor-intensive probes. And with fewer reporters to go around, news outlets are much more likely to abolish investigative slots than the City Hall and police beats.

In the army of the Fourth Estate [the press], full-time investigative reporters have always been the elite special forces. Frequently, though, investigations have been carried out by the foot soldiers—beat reporters who come across a good lead and lobby for permission to pursue it. Decades ago at the *Philadelphia Inquirer* under Executive Editor Gene Roberts, when the paper was known as a prize-winning machine, only Barlett and Steele were detailed to full-time investigations. Says Roberts, "If there was anyone who came up with a good story, they had a reasonable chance of pursuing it at the *Inquirer*, and you did not have to be part of a team."

But fewer and fewer foot soldiers are on patrol.

In 1999, Tom Brune joined *Newsday*'s Washington bureau to cover the U.S. Justice Department and do investigations. With a dozen or more reporters in the office, he had time to look into racial disparity in death row prosecutions, post-9/11 anti-terrorism strategies and relations between Muslim communities and law enforcement. Today, Brune *is* the Washington bureau, holed up in an 8-by-8 office in the E.W. Scripps suite. When I spoke to him, he had spent 12 of the previous 14 days reporting on the Times Square bomber. "Last year I don't think I even came close to a project," he says. . . .

A Bright Spot on the Horizon

While the overall picture may be dismal, there is one very bright spot on the horizon: the rise of nonprofit news outlets committed to investigative reporting. Alarmed by the decline at established media organizations, foundations and other philanthropists have moved to fill the void.

Herbert and Marion Sandler, California banking billionaires with a history of supporting liberal causes, launched ProPublica in 2008 with a pledge of up to $30 million over three years; they hired former *Wall Street Journal* Managing Editor Paul Steiger to run it. Steiger in turn lured Stephen Engelberg from Portland's *Oregonian* to be managing editor of the new venture, and they filled a newsroom in Manhattan's financial district with a mixture of veteran reporters and promising newcomers.

Meanwhile, two existing nonprofits, the Center for Public Integrity [CPI] in Washington, D.C., and the Center for Investigative Reporting [CIR] in Berkeley, [California] are experiencing growth spurts. CPI is known for strip mining databases for story leads. And a track record filled with powerful stories based on the data they contain has given the center credibility. Says Executive Director Bill Buzenberg, a former vice president of National Public Radio, "We love databases no one else has looked at."

CIR is headed by Robert J. Rosenthal, a onetime editor of the *Philadelphia Inquirer* who in 2007 left his post as managing editor of the *San Francisco Chronicle* over the issue of staff cutbacks. Under his leadership, CIR has spun off a regional investigative operation called California Watch with a staff of 17, including 11 reporters. For an editor turned fundraiser, Rosenthal has proved to be a rainmaker, raising some $6.5 million in 18 months.

In addition, a dozen or so smaller operations around the country, such as Voice of San Diego, Texas Watchdog, the New England Center for Investigative Reporting and the Wisconsin Center for Investigative Journalism, have sprung up as hard-hitting local journalism has declined at many traditional media outlets. . . .

Difficult to Count and Track Down

Unlike beat or bureau reporters, investigative journalists are difficult to count. They often are people on beats. In one effort, students at Arizona State University queried the country's hundred largest newspapers in 2006 and found that just 39 percent had an investigative or project team. Of the 61 percent that didn't, 16 percent said there had been one in the past. Thirty-seven percent reported they had no full-time reporters devoted to projects or investigations. Sixty-two percent had no editor charged with overseeing investigations.

In 2008, thinking to update the Arizona survey, Brant Houston, a former IRE executive director who holds the Knight Chair in Investigative and Enterprise Reporting at the University of Illinois, polled the country's 50 largest papers by e-mail. He believed that documenting the attrition in I-Teams might entice foundations to finance the rising crop of non-profits. But answers were hard to come by in an environment ravaged by downsizing.

When he followed up his initial query, Houston sometimes discovered that his contact was no longer employed. Others wanted confidentiality, fearing that "if they pointed out what was happening, they'd be laid off or fired." He was able to establish that at 20 papers, more than half had eliminated or reduced the ranks of investigative reporters. Summarizing his work in [the literary journal] *Daedalus* last spring, he noted that the *Rocky Mountain News* had just folded and the *Seattle Post-Intelligencer* had pared back to a much smaller online operation. Both papers had been known for their strong commitment to investigative journalism.

When a local TV station wants to cut expenses, a distinguished record is no protection. In a long career as an investigative reporter in both local and network news, Roberta Baskin reaped some 75 awards. She was perhaps best known for a 1996 report on the CBS newsmagazine *48 Hours* detailing [sportswear giant] Nike's exploitation of workers in Vietnam. After Baskin protested against news and sportscasters wearing the Nike Swoosh on their jackets while broadcasting the Nike-sponsored 1998 Olympics, she was demoted to CBS' morning program. She moved on to ABC and then spent a year with Bill Moyers at PBS before WJLA wooed her back to the place where she had started out in Washington some 20 years earlier.

The duPont-Columbia award she received on the eve of her dismissal from WJLA was for a report titled "Digging for Dollars," an exposé of a chain of pediatric dental clinics that preyed on Medicaid children. Acting on a tip, Baskin discovered weeping children strapped to "papoose boards" as they underwent root canals and other unnecessary procedures while their parents were kept in the waiting room. The chain eventually settled a suit with the U.S. Justice Department for $24 million.

Many of Baskin's stories began with tips, and some viewers continue to track her down in her current post as senior communications adviser in the Department of Health and Human Service's Office of Inspector General. "I don't know how they find me." . . .

"Investigative Reporting Is Going to Die"

Older, more experienced and better paid, investigative reporters are often the first to go in a downsizing. The lucky ones . . . are offered buyouts. Joe Demma was not so fortunate. A veteran of *Newsday*, where he was an editor or reporter on three Pulitzer-winning stories, Demma had been at Fort Lauderdale's *Sun-Sentinel* for four years, supervising an investigative team of four reporters, when he got the bad news. It was a Friday in July 2008, and he and his wife were preparing for a road trip. Demma was in his office when his boss at the Tribune Co.–owned paper came in and told him layoffs were coming the following week. "I just want you to know your job has been terminated." Demma told his staff and canceled the trip. He was 65, and with just seven weeks of severance pay, money was an issue. "I had to figure out what I was going to do with my life."

Demma looked for a job both inside and outside the news business for two years after he left the paper. Nobody cared about the three Pulitzers on his résumé. He did a stint for the U.S. Census Bureau. It reminded him of when he was a young reporter, "knocking on doors and asking people questions they didn't want to answer." Today he works for a company that publishes corporate histories. "A sentence is a sentence. Put a few of them together and you get a paragraph."

A pronounced decrease in Pulitzer entries for investigative probes suggests the degree to which papers are abandoning the genre. From 1985 to 2010, entries in the investigative category dropped 21 percent, from 103 to 81; in the public service category, the decline was an even steeper 43 percent, from 122 to 70; and for the explanatory category, where investigative work often surfaces, the drop was also 43 percent, from 181 to 104.

A similar decline has taken place in entries for USC Annenberg's $35,000 Selden Ring Award. Since 2005, when there were 88 applications, the number has fallen nearly every year, to 64 in 2010. IRE contest entries also have dropped, from 563 in 2005 to 455 in 2009. Administrators for the Worth Bingham and Goldsmith awards report their numbers are holding steady. . . .

After Tom Dubocq took a buyout at Cox's *Palm Beach Post*, a defense attorney told him his investigative skills were worth money. Lawyers could no longer get the information they used to find in newspapers. [Today], Dubocq is a private investigator. A client might be a creditor who wants a run-down on his debtor's true financial resources, or a company doing due diligence on a potential business partner. Says Dubocq, "I get hired to find the money. I'm pretty good at it."

Mc Nelly Torres had worked at four newspapers by the time she landed at the *Sun-Sentinel* as she followed her husband, who was in the Army, from base to base. Her stories about a string of unsolved female murders in Comanche County, Oklahoma, prompted an FBI investigation; in South Carolina she wrote about industrial hog farms that skirted the law; as the education reporter for the *San Antonio Express-News*, she covered four school districts where there was an abundance of waste and corruption. When she was laid off, she was covering issues related to gasoline sales, consumption and regulation.

She considers accountability journalism her calling. "Not everyone can do this," Torres says. "Not everybody likes to look at thousands of pages that make no sense. But I do."

Torres recently turned down an offer from a large daily. "I don't want to go back to a newspaper. They're not safe."

Instead she is laying the groundwork for a new nonprofit, the Florida Center for Investigative Reporting, dedicated to the kind of work she has done all her life. A major grant recently came through that will help with a fall launch. "If we don't do anything about this," she says, "investigative reporting is going to die."

| *"Collaborations between established media and new groups undertaking investigative journalism have already resulted in revelations whose publication has been in the public interest."*

Investigative Journalism Will Survive

Naomi Westland

In the following viewpoint, Naomi Westland contends that investigative journalism can survive in the mainstream media with the support of investigative news organizations. She suggests that newspapers and external organizations can collaborate to publish investigative stories, with the latter carrying out the reporting. Westland concludes that public interest in investigative journalism still exists and that news organizations must push to publish these stories. Naomi Westland is a journalist and press officer at Amnesty International UK.

As you read, consider the following questions:

1. How does Westland describe the new organizations that are only committed to investigative journalism?

2. In Oliver Wright's view, as cited by the author, what are the benefits of a newspaper's collaborating with an investigative organization?

3. What "third-approach" in investigative journalism is gaining attention, according to Westland?

Investigations by journalists into the conduct of those who hold power are essential to a fully functioning democracy. But investigative journalism is expensive at a time when newspaper budgets are declining. In such an environment, the ability of journalists working for mainstream news organisations to carry out investigations could be at risk.

Evidence presented to the Lords Communications Select Committee on the future of investigative journalism in November [2011] showed that news organisations are committed to investigations, but money, increasing workloads and legal constraints threaten to limit what they can do.

To fill this gap, new organisations whose sole purpose is to carry out journalistic investigations have emerged. While they operate in the same legal framework as mainstream news outlets, they have more time to spend on in-depth investigations than journalists in pressured newsrooms.

A New Collaboration

An investigation exposing the influence political lobbyists have over elected politicians has been published by the [London newspaper the] *Independent*. The investigation was carried out by reporters at The Bureau of Investigative Journalism (TBIJ)—an organisation funded by philanthropic donations which sells and places content to print and broadcast media.

TBIJ is based on a similar model to ProPublica in the US, which according to its website is an "independent, non-profit newsroom that produces investigative journalism in the public interest". Led by Paul Steiger, former managing editor of the *Wall Street Journal*, ProPublica was set up because "investigative journalism is at risk" due to time and budget constraints in the mainstream media and the revolution in publishing technology. It is also funded through philanthropic donations, and brings in some advertising revenue.

Iain Overton, managing editor of TBIJ, explained that having conducted an investigation into the practices of political lobbyists, he spoke to a number of publications to try to get the story placed: "I wanted to feel the editor was really buying into the story because it needed more than one day's coverage. The *Independent* said it would give the story the platform it needed," he said.

The *Independent* didn't pay for the story. Rather it was a trade off: "It's a small paper with a small budget," said Overton, who has previously worked as an investigative journalist for the BBC and ITV, "They gave us the space and we gave them the story."

Oliver Wright, the *Independent*'s Whitehall [where the British government is located] editor, said that there are benefits for newspapers in working with an organisation like TBIJ. He said: "Both sides can bring something important to the story," "They can dig deep and spend more time on a story, and we bring the editorial, contextual and legal side."

He said that stories from external organisations are scrutinised in exactly the same way as those produced internally: "You go through it with a fine-tooth comb with the lawyers, asking the reporter questions about the information".

Wright was keen to point out that these collaborations are not just about money: "Newspapers should be trying to think about what stories they can do and who they can do them with. They can fall into the trap of being proprietorial about their work but we are keen to work together with other organisations," he said.

This type of joint effort was apparent in a recent story—a major collaboration between the *Guardian* and the London School of Economics on the summer riots.

The Future of Investigative Journalism

The future of investigative journalism is likely to lie along at least three paths. On the one hand, in a new media world of information overload where "anyone can be a journalist", investigative journalism offers a way for the mainstream media to provide a distinctive product and prevent the readership migrating elsewhere online. News organisations with declining budgets but a commitment to public service may be inclined to outsource part of their investigative work, taking advantage of their brand and experience and using crowdsourcing approaches to pursue investigative journalism. Finally, and perhaps more realistically, it is likely that foundations and reader donations will increasingly support investigative journalism as an important contribution to society.

Paul Bradshaw, Investigative Journalism, *2008.*

Overton says that while investigations into celebrities can sell papers, a sustainable model for investigating financial institutions, companies and politicians has yet to be discovered: "At the moment it makes no more economic sense to spend 12 hours or three months on a story, as there is no tangible evidence that longer investigations boosts sales, unless they are about celebrities," he said.

Commercial Funding

Another new company specialising in investigative journalism but working on a different funding model is Exaro News. Based in Fleet Street [the traditional area of London where national newspaper offices were located], it is funded by private finance and set to become a subscription-only service in the next month.

Hoping to attract a business audience of city professionals and high-end consumers, Exaro investigates "issues that are important to business in particular and to the public in general, but which are being inadequately covered—or ignored—by the mainstream media", according to its website.

Editor-in-Chief Mark Watts, who has worked for a number of national newspapers as well as for the BBC's *World in Action* and other current affairs programmes, said that of the new investigative organisations that have emerged in the last couple of years, Exaro is the first to attempt it on a commercial footing. "It's very early days but the funders were very keen [interested] because it is innovative," he said. "We are a media organisation in our own right and publish our own work."

The third approach that is gaining profile is investigative journalism funded and carried out by non-governmental organisations [NGOs] with related expertise.

Some NGOs have a budget to carry out investigations. The expertise such organisations have can be valuable, but journalists need to be aware that in certain cases they may have a specific agenda to further their cause.

What the Public Wants

While the news industry has gone through a "McDonalds-ification", said Watts, there is still an appetite among the general public for investigative journalism, and the mainstream newspapers are still carrying out their own investigations: "Some newspapers are churning out celebrity drivel and the public is lapping it up, and the more the public laps it up the more it gets produced. However, the interest and fascination among readers over the MPs [members of Parliament] expenses scandal [exposed by London daily newspaper the *Telegraph*] was palpable".

This was a triumph for the *Telegraph*, said Watts, and boosted sales over the month the story ran. Likewise, the public would never have known about phone hacking at the *News of the World* if it wasn't for the *Guardian* sticking doggedly with a long investigation.

Collaborations between established media and new groups undertaking investigative journalism have already resulted in revelations whose publication has been in the public interest. Such collaborations point the way to a future in which the sourcing and distribution of information may be a joint effort, rather than the sole preserve of what has traditionally been regarded as the fourth estate.

Periodical and Internet Sources Bibliography

The following articles have been selected to supplement the diverse views presented in this chapter.

Belinda Alzner	"It's Time to Kill Investigative Journalism," Canadian Journalism Project, February 24, 2012. http://j-source.ca.
Jeff Bercovici	"Forget That Survey. Here's Why Journalism Is the Best Job Ever," *Forbes*, April 16, 2012.
The Economist	"Newspapers: The Strange Survival of Ink," June 10, 2010.
Gabrielle Kratsas	"Reinventing the News for a Mobile World," *American Journalism Review*, June/July 2013.
Aleks Krotoski	"What Effect Has the Internet Had on Journalism?," *Guardian* (Manchester, UK), February 19, 2011.
Omar Lozano	"Investigative Journalism in Decline in U.S.," Borderzine, August 27, 2010. http://borderzine.com.
Amy Mitchell, Tom Rosenstiel, Laura Houston Santhanam, and Leah Christian	"Future of Mobile News," Pew Research Journalism Project, October 1, 2012. www.journalism.org.
Dan Mitchell	"Where the Web Has Failed Journalism," *Fortune*, March 21, 2013.
Andrea Peterson	"Here's What You Miss by Only Talking to White Men About the Digital Revolution and Journalism," *Washington Post*, September 10, 2013.
Andre Vltchek	"The Death of Investigative Journalism," *CounterPunch*, March 16–18, 2012.

For Further Discussion

Chapter 1

1. In his viewpoint, Theodore Dawes asserts that it is illogical to provide contrasting perspectives about a subject, because this practice is based on the assumption that the truth exists somewhere between the two perspectives. However, in his viewpoint, Aidan White suggests that newsrooms are capable of discerning disputed facts. In your opinion, which author offers the more persuasive argument? Why?

2. In his viewpoint, Greg Marx maintains that undercover journalism often relies on unethical practices. In your view, does the undercover journalism that Brooke Kroeger praises in her viewpoint involve such activities? Use examples from the viewpoints to explain your answer.

3. The authors of the National Summit to Fight Plagiarism & Fabrication state in their viewpoint that plagiarism is a journalistic transgression that betrays the public's trust. In his viewpoint, Paul Farhi insists that errors in journalism are at their highest rate ever. In your opinion, which is a more urgent problem? Why?

Chapter 2

1. In his viewpoint, Chris Hogg claims that one concern about citizen journalists is that they are not held to the same standards and principles that professional journalists are. In your view, does this call into question the successes and integrity of the citizen journalists that Eugene L. Meyer describes in his viewpoint? Why or why not?

2. Michael Tracey argues in his viewpoint that most journalism school graduates do not pursue the profession or work in the news media, therefore journalism degrees

have little purpose. Do you agree or disagree? Why? Cite from the viewpoints in your answer.

3. In his viewpoint, Trevor Butterworth contends that journalism should not be supported as a public service and criticizes news agencies for their lack of strategic and innovative ideas in digital media. Do you agree or disagree? Use examples from the viewpoint to support your answer.

Chapter 3

1. In their viewpoint, David B. Rivkin Jr. and Lee A. Casey contend that a federal shield law is necessary because journalists and reporters rely on anonymous sources. In contrast, Walter Pincus argues in his viewpoint that a federal shield law would encourage the government to target journalists with certain organizational or political ties. In your opinion, which viewpoint provides the more compelling argument? Use examples from the viewpoints to explain your answer.

2. Steve Coll states in his viewpoint that the administration of President Barack Obama has taken unprecedented measures to restrict the free speech rights of journalists. But Michael Kinsley accuses journalists of exploiting the Freedom of Information Act (FOIA) and a reporter's privilege to investigate the government. In your opinion, which author makes the stronger case? Use examples from the viewpoints to support your answer.

Chapter 4

1. In his viewpoint, Tom Rosenstiel contends that the Internet's impact on journalism is misperceived in five ways. In your view, do any of these misperceptions apply to Paul Grabowicz's viewpoint? Use examples from the viewpoints to explain your answer.

2. Alex S. Jones writes in his viewpoint that in order to survive, a newspaper must publish news that is innovative, provocative, and indispensable. Do you agree or disagree? Why?

3. Mary Walton acknowledges in her viewpoint that independent organizations have begun to support the work of investigative journalists. In your opinion, does this weaken her argument that investigative journalism will not survive the rapidly changing media? Why or why not?

Organizations to Contact

The editors have compiled the following list of organizations concerned with the issues debated in this book. The descriptions are derived from materials provided by the organizations. All have publications or information available for interested readers. The list was compiled on the date of publication of the present volume; names, addresses, phone and fax numbers, and e-mail and Internet addresses may change. Be aware that many organizations take several weeks or longer to respond to inquiries, so allow as much time as possible.

American Civil Liberties Union (ACLU)
125 Broad St., 18th Fl., New York, NY 10004
(212) 549-2500
website: www.aclu.org

Founded in 1920, the American Civil Liberties Union is a national, nonprofit, nonpartisan organization that works to defend and protect individual rights as set forth in the US Constitution of the United States. The ACLU publishes several handbooks, public policy reports, project reports, civil liberties books, and pamphlets.

American Copy Editors Society (ACES)
7 Avenida Vista Grande, Ste. B7, #467, Santa Fe, NM 87508
e-mail: info@copydesk.org
website: www.copydesk.org

Founded in 1997, the American Copy Editors Society (ACES) is a nonprofit educational and membership organization for editors working in all areas of publishing, such as newspapers, magazines, books, websites, and other digital media. Members include traditionally employed editors as well as freelancers. The society also offers membership to students and educators of journalism, English, and communications. The ACES aims to provide solutions to editing problems, professional training, and a place for members to discuss common issues. The society holds a well-attended, three-day convention every year that offers various workshops, panel discussions, and networking opportunities.

American Society of Magazine Editors (ASME)
575 Third Ave., 11th Fl., New York, NY   10017
(212) 872-3700 • fax: (212) 906-0128
e-mail: asme@magazine.org
website: www.magazine.org/asme

Founded in 1963, the American Society of Magazine Editors is the principal organization for magazine journalists in the United States. The members of ASME include the editorial leaders of most major print and online magazines. ASME works to defend the First Amendment, protect editorial independence, and support the development of journalism. The society sponsors the National Magazine Awards in association with the Columbia Journalism School and publishes *ASME Guidelines for Editors and Publishers*.

Center for Investigative Reporting (CIR)
1400 Sixty-Fifth St., Ste. 200, Emeryville, CA   94608
(510) 809-3160 • fax: (510) 652-1792
e-mail: info@cironline.org
website: http://cironline.org

Founded in 1977, CIR is a nonprofit news organization composed of journalists dedicated to encouraging investigative reporting. It conducts investigations, offers consulting services to news and special-interest organizations, and conducts workshops and seminars for investigative journalists. Its publications include blogs, numerous reporting guides, and investigative reports on contemporary topics and issues.

Fairness and Accuracy in Reporting (FAIR)
112 W. Twenty-Seventh St., New York, NY   10001
(212) 633-6700 • fax: (212) 727-7668

e-mail: fair@fair.org
website: http://fair.org

Founded in 1986, FAIR is a national media watchdog group that offers documented criticism of media bias and censorship. The group contends that the media are controlled by corporate and governmental interests and are insensitive to women, labor, minorities, and other special-interest groups. FAIR publishes the bimonthly magazine, *Extra!* and produces the weekly radio show, *CounterSpin.*

Freedom Forum
555 Pennsylvania Ave. NW, Washington, DC   20001
(202) 292-6100
e-mail: news@freedomforum.org
website: www.freedomforum.org

Founded in 1991, Freedom Forum is a nonpartisan research organization dedicated to studying the media and educating the public about the media's influence on society. It publishes an annual report, as well as publications on free speech, freedom of information, newsroom diversity, and media ethics.

National Association of Black Journalists (NABJ)
1100 Knight Hall, Ste. 3100, College Park, MD   20742
(301) 405-0248 • fax: (301) 314-1714
website: www.nabj.org

Founded in 1975, the National Association of Black Journalists is the largest organization of journalists of color in the United States. It works to strengthen ties among African American journalists, promote diversity in newsrooms, and honor the achievements of black journalists. The NABJ holds an annual convention that includes a career fair and workshops for professional development. It also publishes the quarterly *NABJ Journal.*

National Newspaper Association (NNA)
PO Box 50301, Arlington, VA   22205

(703) 237-9802 • fax: (703) 237-9808
website: http://nnaweb.org

Established in 1885, the National Newspaper Association is a nonprofit trade association representing newspapers across the United States. Its mission is to protect, promote, and enhance America's community newspapers, including daily, nondaily, online, college, church, and neighborhood newspapers. The NNA website offers research on trends affecting the industry and views on public policies that impact newspapers.

Pew Research Journalism Project
1615 L St. NW, Ste. 700, Washington, DC   20036
(202) 419-3650 • fax: (202) 419-3699
e-mail: journalism@pewresearch.org
website: www.journalism.org

Founded in 1997, the Pew Research Journalism Project of the Pew Research Center, is a nonpartisan organization that conducts public opinion polls, researches demographics, and analyzes media content in order to inform the public about attitudes, issues, and trends that are shaping the United States and the rest of the world. The journalism project is researching the media and analyzing data to see whether consumers are getting the information they need to make decisions and live their lives. The areas the project studies include who is delivering the news, what type of news is being reported, what information is not being reported, and how consumers choose to receive news. The project's website provides analyses, a data library, and a content index on news coverage. The Pew Research Journalism Project also publishes the annual report *State of the News Media.*

Radio Television Digital News Association (RTDNA)
National Press Bldg., Washington, DC   20045
fax: (202) 223-4007
website: www.rtdna.org

Founded in 1946, the Radio Television Digital News Association is the world's largest professional organization serving the electronic news profession. Its members include news directors, news associates, educators, and students. The RTDNA is dedicated to setting standards for news gathering and reporting. Its website provides information about ethics, best practices, social media, and technology.

Reporters Committee for Freedom of the Press (RCFP)
1101 Wilson Blvd., Ste. 1100, Arlington, VA   22209
(800) 336-4243
e-mail: info@rcfp.org
website: www.rcfp.org

Founded in 1970, the Reporters Committee for Freedom of the Press is a nonprofit organization that provides free legal assistance to journalists. Its mission is to protect the right to gather and report news; to ensure access to public records, meetings, and courtrooms; and to preserve the First Amendment right to free speech. RCPF publications include *The First Amendment Handbook* and the online resource "Digital Journalist's Legal Guide." Both are available on the organization's website.

Society of Professional Journalists (SPJ)
Eugene S. Pulliam National Journalism Center
Indianapolis, IN   46208
(317) 927-8000 • fax: (317) 920-4789
website: www.spj.org

Founded in 1909, the Society of Professional Journalists is a nonprofit professional organization for journalists. Members include broadcast, print, and online journalists as well as journalism students and educators. The SPJ is dedicated to promoting the flow of information, protecting the First Amendment, supporting high standards and ethical behavior in the practice of journalism, and fostering excellence among journalists.

Bibliography of Books

Stuart Allan

Citizen Witnessing: Revisioning Journalism in Times of Crisis. Malden, MA: Polity, 2013.

David E. Boeyink and Sandra L. Borden

Making Hard Choices in Journalism Ethics: Cases and Practice. New York: Routledge, 2010.

M. Grazia Busà

Introducing the Language of the News: A Student's Guide. Hoboken, NJ: Taylor & Francis, 2013.

W. Joseph Campbell

Getting It Wrong: Ten of the Greatest Misreported Stories in American Journalism. Berkeley: University of California Press, 2010.

Stephanie Craft and Charles N. Davis

Principles of American Journalism: An Introduction. New York: Routledge, 2013.

Christopher B. Daly

Covering America: A Narrative History of a Nation's Journalism. Amherst: University of Massachusetts Press, 2012.

David Folkenflik, ed.

Page One: Inside the "New York Times" and the Future of Journalism. New York: PublicAffairs, 2011.

Kathy Roberts Forde

Literary Journalism on Trial: Masson v. New Yorker *and the First Amendment.* Amherst: University of Massachusetts Press, 2008.

| Jack Fuller | *What Is Happening to News: The Information Explosion and the Crisis in Journalism.* Chicago: University of Chicago Press, 2010. |

| Jennifer George-Palilonis | *The Multimedia Journalist: Storytelling for Today's Media Landscape.* New York: Oxford University Press, 2013. |

| Juan González and Joseph Torres | *News for all the People: The Epic Story of Race and the American Media.* New York: Verso, 2011. |

| Shanto Iyengar and Donald R. Kinder | *News That Matters: Television and American Opinion.* Updated ed. Chicago: University of Chicago Press, 2010. |

| George Kennedy and Daryl Moen, eds. | *What Good Is Journalism? How Reporters and Editors Are Saving America's Way of Life.* Columbia: University of Missouri Press, 2007. |

| Janet Kolodzy | *Practicing Convergence Journalism: An Introduction to Cross-Media Storytelling.* New York: Routledge, 2013. |

| Bill Kovach and Tom Rosenstiel | *Blur: How to Know What's True in the Age of Information Overload.* New York: Bloomsbury, 2010. |

| Bill Kovach and Tom Rosenstiel | *The Elements of Journalism: What Newspeople Should Know and the Public Should Expect.* New York: Three Rivers, 2007. |

Paul McCaffrey, ed.	*The News and Its Future.* New York: Wilson, 2010.
Steven Maras	*Objectivity in Journalism.* Malden, MA: Polity, 2013.
Robert W. McChesney and Victor Pickard	*Will the Last Reporter Please Turn Out the Lights: The Collapse of Journalism and What Can Be Done to Fix It.* New York: New Press, 2011.
Missouri Group, Brian S. Brooks, Daryl R. Moen, Don Ranley, and George Kennedy	*Telling the Story: The Convergence of Print, Broadcast and Online Media.* 5th ed. Boston: Bedford/St. Martin's, 2013.
Roger Patching and Martin Hirst	*Journalism Ethics: Arguments and Cases for the Twenty-First Century.* New York: Routledge, 2013.
Norman Pearlstine	*Off the Record: The Press, the Government, and the War over Anonymous Sources.* New York: Farrar, Straus & Giroux, 2007.
Chris Peters and M.J. Broersma, eds.	*Rethinking Journalism: Trust and Participation in a Transformed News Landscape.* New York: Routledge, 2013.
Michael Schudson	*The Sociology of News.* 2nd ed. New York: Norton, 2012.
Rodger Streitmatter	*Mightier than the Sword: How the News Media Have Shaped American History.* 3rd ed. Boulder, CO: Westview, 2012.

| Debora Halpern Wenger and Deborah Potter | *Advancing the Story: Broadcast Journalism in a Multimedia World.* 2nd ed. Washington, DC: CQ Press, 2012. |

Index